2006年宁波市教育科学规划课题成果
（项目名称：词汇理据与词汇教学研究）

2010年教育部人文社会科学研究一般项目（青年基金）成果
（项目名称：应用科学知识图谱的外语学科30年发展研究，
项目批准号：10YJC740039）

外语·文化·教学论丛

A Study of Lexical Motivations and Lexis Teaching

词汇理据与词汇教学研究

吴会芹 胡海鹏 施亚波 李 辉 著

图书在版编目（CIP）数据

词汇理据与词汇教学研究／吴会芹等著．—杭州：浙江大学出版社，2011.8
ISBN 978-7-308-08855-8

Ⅰ．①词… Ⅱ．①吴… Ⅲ．①英语—词汇学—研究②英语—词汇—教学研究 Ⅳ．①H313

中国版本图书馆 CIP 数据核字（2011）第 134526 号

词汇理据与词汇教学研究

吴会芹　胡海鹏　施亚波　李　辉　著

责任编辑　朱　玲
文字编辑　徐　瑾
封面设计　刘依群
出版发行　浙江大学出版社
（杭州市天目山路 148 号　邮政编码 310007）
（网址：http://www.zjupress.com）
排　　版　杭州中大图文设计有限公司
印　　刷　浙江云广印业有限公司
开　　本　710mm×1000mm　1/16
印　　张　14.25
字　　数　260 千
版 印 次　2011 年 8 月第 1 版　2011 年 8 月第 1 次印刷
书　　号　ISBN 978-7-308-08855-8
定　　价　30.00 元

浙江大学出版社发行部邮购电话　(0571)88925591

前 言

“字词的构成理据是一个值得探讨的话题。字词的构成是以任意性为重还是以理据性为重也是语言学界长期讨论并存在争议的问题。以此话题为研究对象的论文颇具挑战性。近年来,国内语言学界过多地强调了语言的象似性特征而忽略了索绪尔的任意性学说。任意性是符号的一般特征,具有复合型的一般性理论意义。语言符号的任意性是一般符号任意性的一种佐证。基础语言符号是任意性的,而语言的理据则体现在规则中。符号的任意性实质在于,其所指因认知方式不同而有差异,其能指具有更多的不确定性。本文研究的范围仅限于英语新词的语义理据而非原始词汇或初创词汇的语义理据,这就缩小了话题的范围,为研究的深入提供了便利。作者认为词汇的理据原则和任意性原则共存,它们都是语言的本质属性。论文分析合理,详略得当,具有一定的深度,为语言学习者提供了可以遵循的构词原则,具有理论指导价值。”

以上是河南大学硕士论文评审专家麻保金教授对我的硕士论文“英语新词的形态理据与语义理据研究”的一段评语。感谢我的导师杨良生教授对我的特别支持。硕士论文撰写过程中我还特别得到了河南大学博士生导师徐有志教授的多次指正,在此谨致诚挚的谢意。美籍教师David B. Gephart为本文的英文文字进行了审阅,在此一同致谢。

本著是在该论文基础上拓展而成的。在后来的拓展工作中我曾得到了浙江大学、浙江大学宁波理工学院多位专家的支持和帮助,并获得2006年宁波市教育科学规划课题立项,项目名称为“词汇理据与词汇教

学研究”。期间施亚波、胡海鹏两位老师分别参与了第七章(包括附录4)、第九章(包括附录6)的撰写工作,但由于当时的条件所限,本书未能及时出版。2010年胡海鹏老师申请的“应用科学知识图谱的外语学科30年发展研究”获教育部人文社会科学研究一般项目(青年基金)资助,在此项目的支撑下,本书的出版事宜终于确定下来。我们在原稿基础上重新整理并修改了一些内容,李辉老师也参与了本书第八章(包括附录5)的撰写工作。

本书能够最终出版得益于上述专家及同事的大力支持和慷慨帮助,在此表示诚挚的谢意。

本书第一章、第二章、第三章、第四章、第五章、第六章、第十章(包括附录1—3)及中英文摘要等内容均由我执笔完成,并负责全书的统稿工作。

吴会芹

2011年5月

Abstract

This book is an attempt to provide multiple perspectives for an approach into the insight of English lexical motivation and lexis teaching.

As a fresh issue in linguistics, motivation study stems from the proposal as principle of arbitrariness made by Saussure. (2001) Hence, it is necessary to clarify the relationship between arbitrariness and motivation of linguistic signs, which is to be a theoretical basis for the issue that follows. For the ultimate goals of the whole book, the issue of the relationship between the two needs clarification before we could get started with the main topic—the study of lexical motivations and lexis teaching. The book on motivations of new English lexis serves as a detailed analysis of lexical motivations, which is in turn to support the theory. It is noted that both the arguments over arbitrariness and motivation, and the study on the issue of motivations reflect cognitive process of human beings. In this sense, cognitive linguistics constitutes another theoretical basis for the whole study.

This book is composed of ten chapters.

Chapter One is a brief introduction to the whole book. This chapter provides with a new definition of motivation, a new classification of

motivations of linguistic signs, an explanation to the conceptual characteristics of motivation, and the framework of the whole book.

Chapter Two gives a brief overview of the process of the arguments over arbitrariness, motivation and iconicity, which indicates a cognitive progress in this book. This argument has come about as a result of Saussure's proposal on the principle of arbitrariness. As to the relationship between arbitrariness and motivation in language study, opinions vary among scholars in different times, which can be concluded as follows: The first one is that linguistic signs are either arbitrary or motivated. Those who hold to this belief that linguistic signs are arbitrary contend that arbitrariness is prior to motivation. Those who are against the arbitrariness of linguistic signs claim that linguistic signs are motivated rather than arbitrary. The second one is that linguistic signs can be classified into two groups, one is arbitrary and the other motivated. The third one is that arbitrariness and motivation are two natures of linguistic signs viewed from different perspectives. On the one hand, linguistic signs themselves share both arbitrariness and motivation; on the other hand, both the two are the different perspectives from which we study linguistic signs. The combination of the three beliefs constitutes a perfect cognitive process. It is noted that the clarification of the relationship between the two concepts will improve, develop and even, to a certain extent, perfect linguistic theories, the most important being Saussure's philosophy of linguistics. In this sense, the purpose of this study is to make a contribution to linguistic theories, and to a certain extent, to fill in a theoretical void in motivation study.

Considering the two natures of linguistic signs, motivation study on English lexis is only the subdivision of the two. The study on lexical motivations is a blend of lexicology and motivation study. On the one hand, motivation study is a fresh issue in linguistics. On the other hand, a single word, in its true sense, is an entity conveying meaning together with its phonation. The fact that the linguistic system was once classified into phonetics, vocabulary and grammar, and then into phonetics, semantics and grammar, and still later into phonetics, vocabulary, semantics and grammar, highly suggests the rich contents and research significance of vocabulary study. In this study, motivations of English lexis will be studied from a large variety of perspectives, supporting the research objective and significance of this study.

Chapter Three overlooks the phonological motivations in English lexis, which mainly contains onomatopoeia, reduplication, phonological change of shifting, and phonemes. In a narrow sense (in phonology), motivation in onomatopoeia can be highly motivated. The fact that there exists a direct relationship between the onomatopoeia and the objective world unquestionably supports the onomatopoeia motivation in words. In a broad sense (compared with morphological and semantic motivations), the phonological motivation in English words is considered very low. This is because written words are considered to be the major form in language recording.

Chapter Four discusses the morphological motivations in English lexis, from both pictographic and word-formational perspectives. The former includes pictographic motivations in capital letters and some English words, in the mixture of pictograph and meaning, in initial pictographs, and in recessive pictographs. The latter involves mostly composition, derivation, abbreviation, backformation, borrowing, coinage, etc., which is conducted mainly by western linguists.

Chapter Five presents a detailed description of semantic

motivations. Semantic motivations extend to a large variety of fields, concerning politics, social events, environment, lifestyle, science and technology, and information science. This part constitutes the most interesting of all, for each new word exemplified, tells an interesting story. Exploration of its semantic motivations arouses the greatest interests of learners, inspiring them to keep a keen eye on both the new words themselves and the rules of word invention to follow.

Chapter Six investigates the lexical motivations from psychological perspectives. As mentioned above, arbitrariness and motivation are both natures of linguistic signs. The former guarantees the creativity and productivity of new lexis, while the latter exhibits the rules for language learners to follow. The process in which English words are invented is completed by imitating the sounds of nature, the images they represent, the characteristics of the images they represent, and the ways some words are created. Psychologically, they are imitational and creative motivations. By investigating the psychological motivations of imitation or creation in inventing new words, we may not only reveal some rules to follow in creating words, but also help learners to memorize new words in a more effective and efficient way. In this sense, this study is of great significance to language teaching and learning.

Chapter Seven presents a detailed study of etymological motivations of new English lexis. Etymological motivations means that the meaning of word is directly related to its etymology, that is, the origin of word determines its current meaning. The study of etymology can be divided into three parts: the origin of words; the change of the form and meaning of words; the motivation of words. It involves not only the origin, meaning and change of words, but also focuses on the internal causes and hidden reasons. Seven sources of etymological motivations are discussed in great detail.

Chapter Eight provides psychological motivations by employing a word association test, aiming at investigating the nature of Chinese English learners' mental lexicon by comparing the association responses of native speakers and Chinese English learners. The result shows that there are significant differences in the structure of mental lexicons between Chinese English learners and native speakers. With regard to L1 mental lexicons, Chinese English learners have poorer concentricity of association and weaker association strength. Their association is more dependent on forms. They have no established systematic and stable networks between words. The semantic network in their mental lexicon is underdeveloped.

The experimental results give some clues and help to L2 vocabulary teaching. In college English teaching, teachers are supposed to organize some activities and exercises to help students construct semantic association networks. What's more, they need increase L2 language input, systematically explain word formation, improve students' mental lexicon knowledge and avoid using translation teaching method.

Chapter Nine studies the application of motivation for students' vocabulary acquisition in multimedia environment. It involves the application of audio, vision, and video information input to learn English vocabulary.

It gives a brief introduction to current situation of vocabulary learning and teaching in China and abroad, and then introduces vocabulary acquisition with CALL and CALT, together with psychological and multimedia hardware and software foundation for vocabulary learning. The second part is for the computational application of vocabulary acquisition, especially the application of corpus database.

Last but not least, this chapter proposes several suggestions on vocabulary learning and teaching.

The last chapter ends up with the conclusion.

Firstly, linguistic signs are both arbitrary and motivated. Secondly, new English lexis is highly motivated. Thirdly, new English lexis tends to be more casual, more abbreviated, more various, and more influential. It is the advantage or superiority in science and technology that makes the language speaking nation more powerful, thus making its language more influential, regardless of its history.

By exploring morphological and semantic motivations in words, vocabulary problems for second language learners can be partly solved. On the one hand, a morphological motivation provides learners with some rules to follow, creating a link between the well-known words and words not yet known, so that the well-known may remind the learners of the new. On the other hand, semantic motivations enable the learners to be more interested in vocabulary learning, for each tells an interesting story. If we can achieve the goal of increasing vocabulary by exploring lexical motivations, we will feel well rewarded.

Key words: linguistic signs; arbitrariness; motivation; lexical motivation; vocabulary teaching

摘　要

理据研究在语言学领域中尚属一个新课题，它的提出缘于索绪尔的任意性原则，因此，在探讨理据问题之前有必要澄清任意性与理据性的关系，这将为词汇理据的研究提供必要的理论依据。也就是说，只有理清任意性与理据性的关系，才能从正确的角度进行词汇理据问题研究。研究英语新词的理据将为上述理论提供充分的立论依据。一个不容忽视的问题是，任意性与理据性的关系的争论过程反映了人类复杂的认知过程，对词汇理据的研究亦是如此。正因如此，认知语言学也将作为本书的另一理论基础。

本书共分十章。

第一章是对理据问题的概述。本章阐释了理据的概念、理据的分类以及词汇理据研究所牵涉的层面。

首先，笔者参照理据研究专家史蒂芬·乌尔曼和严辰松教授对理据的分类，提出其分类法具有一定的偏颇和重叠等不妥之处，并在此基础上对理据进行重新分类，即语言理据可分为内部理据和外部理据两大板块，内部理据包括语音理据、形态理据和语义理据，而外部理据则是一个开放性的范围，它可以从语言外部各个角度加以阐释。

其次，笔者依据上述分类对理据的概念特征进行分析，发现理据具有三个重要特征。一、理据具有线性特征，指语言符号背后的故事。它是语言符号产生的源泉，是促成语言符号产生的直接或间接动因。二、理据具

有塔状性特征。当一个语言符号浅层意义上的理据被挖掘出来后，这种同类意义、相似构词形式的语言符号便产生了家族性、象似性的聚合群。三、理据具有发散性特征。从认知学角度讲，就是语言符号自身的范畴化过程；从心理学角度讲，就是人类对语言符号的模仿与复制过程；从文体学角度讲，就是人类对语言符号进行类推创造的过程。这一过程产生的含有多项或类似结构、类似构词、类似构形的语言符号群是一个具有语义（构词/构形）层次的聚合体，其中，上义语言符号是有理据的，而横向层面上的下义符号则体现着相对的任意性。

第二章回顾自索绪尔提出语言符号任意性原则，以及由此引发的在语言学界长达半个多世纪的语言符号任意性与理据性、理据性与象似性之争论。这一争论过程反映了人类在这一问题研究领域的认知过程。就任意性和理据性的关系而言，长期以来专家学者众说纷纭，归纳起来主要集中在以下三点：第一，语言符号或是任意的，或是有理据的。起初，语言符号任意说占统治地位，持此观点者认为，语言符号是任意的，起码任意性先于理据性。但是，当越来越多的语料证据一遍又一遍地佐证了语言符号是有理据的时候，部分学者开始相信语言符号的理据性，或者认为语言符号的理据性大于任意性。第二，语言符号可以归为两类，一类是任意的，一类是有理据的。第三，任意性和理据性属于语言符号的双个不同属性。一方面，语言符号本身既有任意的特征，同时又具有理据性的一面；另一方面，语言符号的任意性和理据性属于两个不同层面的研究内容。上述三种观点构成了人类对语言理论认知的完美过程，在一定程度上发展、完善了语言学理论，尤其是对探讨索绪尔的语言哲学思想具有重大的理论意义。笔者只想在此汲一杯水于沧海，探一道险于丛林，以其微薄之力，弥补语言学理论浩瀚烟海之一席空白。

针对语言符号的两重属性，理据研究属于其分支学科。而词汇理据研究是集词汇学与理据学研究的综合体。一方面，理据研究是一个新兴学科；另一方面，“词汇”本身是音义结合后具有独立使用价值的一个综合体。语言学科的体系划分从“语音、词汇、语法”的三分，到“语音”、“语义”、“语法”的三分，再到“语音”、“词汇”、“语义”、“语法”的四分的发展历程可以看出，其中交叉错叠、欲弃又取的正是“词汇”。这恰恰体现了词汇本身的丰富性和研究价值。笔者将从英语新词的形态理据及语义理据等方面进行探讨，其选题目的和意义由此窥见一斑。

第三章探讨了英语词汇的语音理据。语音理据主要包括拟声理据、发声理据、叠声理据、重音迁移和音素变化等。从微观角度看，拟声具有极高的理据性，这是因为英语是一个以发音为基础的表音文字系统。毫无疑问，拟声与客观物体之间具有直接关系，这就足以表明词具有拟声理据性。然而，这并不等于所有以声构词的词语含义都由此推导出来。从宏观角度看(与形态理据和语义理据相比较)，词汇的语音理据性较弱。

第四章分别从英语词汇的构词和构形特征方面对英语新词的形态理据进行了探究。英语作为字母体系，对其形态理据的研究主要从构词理据着手，这也是西方语言学家研究词汇的常规方法。英语的构词理据主要有复合、派生、缩略、逆生、借用、新造等。英语词汇的象形理据主要是在借鉴了汉语词汇的象形特征的基础上分析得来的，主要包括大写首字母象形理据以及单词本身形态的象形理据。

第五章详细分析和探讨了英语新词的语义理据。笔者引用了大量的新词语料以及其产生的渊源，对英语新词的语义理据进行归类，发现语义理据牵涉范围非常广泛，有政治、社会、环境、生活方式、科学技术、信息科学等方面的理据。这也是全文中最有趣的内容，因为文中所列举的每一个新单词的背后都隐藏了一段鲜为人知的故事。探讨英语新词的语义理据将会极大地激发学习者的学习兴趣，激发他们以极大的热情关注英语新词汇本身以及造词规律。

第六章将从心理学角度探讨英语词汇的心理理据。如前所述，任意性与理据性是语言符号的两个特性，理据性使语言符号的学习有法可依、有章可循，任意性则是语言符号再生力和创造力的源泉。英语新词再生或创造过程是通过仿拟声音、仿拟形象、仿拟特征、仿拟构词等形式完成的，这些形式反映在人的心理上就是人类通过语言符号对声音、形象、特

征、构词等现象的模拟，即模仿理据。研究英语新词再生过程中的模仿理据既可揭示英语新词的造词规律，又可以帮助语言学习者事半功倍地记忆单词，其教学意义由此窥见一斑。

第七章主要从词源学角度详细探讨了英语词汇的词源理据。词源理据是指词的意义同它们的本源有直接的联系，也就是说词的身世来由可以说明它现今的词义。新词语的词源研究至少包括三个方面：来源、变化及理据。词源研究既要考察词语的出处、意义和变化，又要探讨之所以形成的促动因素。本章主要从历史事件、文学典故、文化习俗、希腊神话、圣经故事、人名地名、外来词等七个方面探讨英语的词源理据。

第八章采用了词汇联想测试方法，通过比较中国英语学习者和母语者的反应词的不同，来探究中国英语学习者二语心理词汇的特点。结果表明：中国英语学习者和母语者的心理词汇结构存在显著差异。与母语者相比，中国英语学习者的联想集中性较差，联想强度较弱；中国英语学习者过分依赖词的形态来联想；词与词之间没有形成系统的、稳固的联系网络；语义网络不完善。

实验结果对二语词汇教学有一定的启示和帮助。在大学二语课堂教学中教师应通过一些活动和练习帮助学生建立语义联系网络；增加二语语言输入；系统讲解英语构词法知识；完善学生二语心理词汇知识；尽量避免使用翻译教学法。

第九章主要介绍了词汇理据在多媒体环境下对学生词汇学习的应用。利用多媒体的声音、图像和录像从多个输入途径对学生词汇学习给予帮助。对于 CALL 和 CALT 的历史和现状做了一定的介绍，其中也包括了其心理基础和计算机软硬件基础。本章介绍了多媒体教学的三个主要特点，以及在多媒体环境下的多种词汇理据应用和一些词汇学习与教学策略。此外，本章还介绍了多媒体环境下利用语料库的词汇理据应用及词汇学习与教学策略。最后就词汇教学及学习提出建议。

最后一章是对全书的总结。

第一，语言符号既是有理据的又是任意的。第二，英语新词具有很强的理据性。第三，理据研究表明，英语新词越来越随意化、缩略化和多样化，其影响范围日益广泛。撇开历史不谈，正是科学技术上的优势才得以使使用本语言的民族更强大，使其语言有更广泛的影响力。

通过探究词汇的理据，令人头疼的词汇问题将会部分地迎刃而解。一方面，形态理据为第二语言学习者提供了可以遵循的构词规则，在熟知和陌生的单词之间建立联想，这样熟悉的成分便可以诱发学习者产生联想，以此帮助记忆生词。另一方面，语义理据可以激发学习者对词汇学习的兴趣，因为每一个新词都讲述了一段有趣的故事。如果我们能通过研究和探讨词汇理据达到帮助第二语言学习者扩充词汇量之目的，笔者将感到由衷地欣慰。

关键词：语言符号；任意性；理据性；词汇理据；词汇教学

CONTENTS

Chapter One Introduction

This chapter gives a brief introduction to the whole study concerning the following issues:

Why did the author choose motivations of new English lexis as her topic?

What is the present situation on the study of this topic?

What will this study aim to achieve?

What is the practical and theoretical significance of this study?

What is motivation?

How's the classification of motivation?

1.1 Brief Introduction to Motivation

For a better understanding of the issue, we need to answer two questions before getting started. First, are linguistic signs arbitrary or motivated? Based on the answer to this question, the question that follow might be: from which perspective can new English lexis be motivated?

Answering the first question involves a literature review concerning the relationship between the arbitrariness and motivation (see Chapter

Two). Regardless of Saussure's explanation, generally speaking, the interpretations over the two fall into three main categories: the either-arbitrary-while-or-motivated one; the some-arbitrary-while-others-motivated one; and the both-arbitrary-and-motivated one.

The fact that interpretations to the principle of arbitrariness vary from individual, indicates that the issue with respect to the relationship between motivation and arbitrariness is quite controversial and meanwhile hard to tackle. The fact that, for nearly half a century, the most intense arguments in linguistic field have been oriented around Saussure's principle of arbitrariness, suffices to explain Saussure's profound influence in the evolution of language studies. For a long period of time, more studies on the issue whether linguistic signs are arbitrary or motivated have been conducted, while little investigation on motivations as an independent issue has been made. As the only work focusing on "motivation", *A Study on Linguistic Motivations* (王艾录，司富珍，2002) is a real find. Unfortunately, most of the samples exemplified are taken from the languages as Chinese, with only a few from ther languages as English. We could hardly find any other English or Chinese versions of motivations of English words, especially of new English lexis. Theoretically speaking, the academic shortage on this issue motivates us to conduct further investigation on the issue of "motivation", the subdivision of the study on arbitrariness.

This limited study tries to investigate the motivations of English lexis, in particular, the new words included in dictionaries within a couple of decades. By examining the morphological motivations of new English lexis, we find the new English lexis not only shares some motivations with English lexis, but also has its unique motivations. Compared with English vocabulary, the new English lexis is more motivated simply because most of the new English words are compounds, loan words and abbreviates, being more highly motivated (王艾录，司富珍，2002；朱永生，2002). Morphological motivations provide learners with some rules to follow, creating a linking association between the well-known and the new, so that the former may remind the learners of the latter. In the process of investigating semantic motivations of new English lexis, we intend to find some rules for English learners to follow. The creation of new English lexis is not only related to man's physical activities but also associated with man's mental activities (see Chapter Five). Semantic motivations help to arouse learners' interests in word building, for each word tells an interesting story. It is for this reason that we conduct the book mainly from morphological and semantic perspectives.

In this book, the main samples were collected from related publications or through the Internet, some of which can be found in new dictionaries, while some can only be found in on-line dictionaries.

As to the criteria of new lexis, we combine the definitions by Lin Cheng-zhang (2005 3rd Edition: 130), Knowles (1998: iii), Mckean (2003: viii-ix) and by an editor of *Merriam-Webster's Collegiate Dictionary*.[①] (2003: 11th Edition) We conclude that neologism or new

---

① As to the time from which on new words appeared, Lin Cheng-zhang (2005 3rd Edition, 130) suggests the period should be "among forty years from the sixties to the late nineties last century". As for what can be called a new word, Knowles E. (1998: iii) defines it "as any word, phrase, or sense that came into popular use or enjoyed a vogue in the given period". Mckean E. (2003: viii-ix) stresses a new word "must earn its place in the dictionary by showing that people are using it—lots of people, in lots of different places". In the eyes of an editor of *Merriam-Webster's Collegiate Dictionary* (11th Edition) published in 2003, "A new word should have been in consistent use for at least ten years before being entered in our dictionary."

lexis refers to any newly coined or existing words, phrases or senses that have been in constant use or have become the vogue since the 1960s. Thus, the samples collected in this study are those that have been emerging into the English vocabulary since the 1960s.

Practically speaking, the burden of learning lexis is the amount of effort needed to learn and memorize. Unfortunately, while making an extra effort to memorize new words they meet, learners often feel helpless and even frustrated. In this case, many teachers, even some scholars have been racking their brains for more effective ways to tackle this problem. Some create a link between the word form and its meaning by imagining an image similar to the word form so that learners may easily associate the form with its spelling (see pictographic motivations). Others bridge a link between a new word and the one they are familiar with, so that the latter one may easily remind the learner of the former. This is because there is a link between the new and the used one. Other possible techniques are to take advantages of affixes and roots (see morphological motivations). Although the techniques mentioned above seem rather bizarre at first, their effectiveness lies in its association that holds between the form and meaning of the new word by using aural and imagery cues. This is why many publications on mnemonic techniques in vocabulary learning, though academically controversial, have been commercially successful. The present situation has inspired our enthusiasm in the study of "lexical motivations".

The study on motivations of English lexis will be helpful, not only in reinforcing a learner's power of memorizing, but also in arousing the interests of learners, for each motivation tells an interesting story about the word. Young students are always ready to accept anything new. As an English teacher in modern society, and hence as a link between the outside world and the students—the young adults with a strong desire to connect, to communicate and to cooperate with the highly developed outside world, he or she should always be alert to anything new, including the new lexis in modern society. It is true that young adults are willing to touch anything new, including new words created in modern times. It is also true that parts of the new lexis, though too new to be listed in any dictionaries, strongly appeal to the younger generation. Choosing new lexis as the topic of the study is the most suitable one for an English teacher of young adults. It is the present situation that motivates to confine this study to "motivations of new English lexis".

Briefly speaking, the study will start with clarifying the relationship between arbitrariness and motivation of linguistic signs, which will direct the study on lexical motivations along a non-biased route (see Chapter Two). As far as the principle of arbitrariness is concerned, people's understandings of it vary from individual to individual. Many interpret "arbitrariness" as that "linguistic signs can be arbitrarily formed, created, and changed as one likes". In our opinion, this hypothesis is arbitrarily and literally distorted, as Saussure's arbitrariness contains the other aspect of this issue—"motivation" (see Chapter Two).

Chapters Three to Five, makes a detailed investigation on phonological, morphological and semantic motivations in English lexis, which constitutes the internal motivations of linguistic signs of English lexis. Chapters Six to Eight is an exploration of lexical motivations from psychological, etymological perspectives, which constitutes the external motivation part of linguistic signs.

Chapters Nine is the practical application of motivation study. Unlike the former chapters, these two chapters take lexis teaching and

lexis acquisition as focus, constituting another independent part of the whole study. The last chapter ends up with a conclusion.

The study on motivations of new English lexis, is not only an attempt to investigate Saussure's theory on general linguistics, but also an extension of Saussure's principle of arbitrariness. The exploration in motivations of English lexis, to a certain extent, will undoubtedly make a clarification of the relationship between the two, and should help to complete, to improve and to develop linguistic theories.

This study is also a contribution to cognitive linguistics, which will elaborate on the three stages of arguments on the relationship between arbitrariness and motivation, providing with a cognitive perspective to the Saussure's philosophy of linguistics. Moreover, the appearance of the term "motivation" marks the gradual developing process of man's cognition in language and thinking patterns (方立, 2001),① indicating there is a cognitive route in the history of linguistic study.

1.2 Theoretical Significance of This Study

The study on motivation of language signs is one aspect of the study on the relationship that holds between arbitrariness and motivation, which was motivated by the principle of arbitrariness proposed by Saussure since his *Course in General Linguistics* was released, particularly since 1960s. Over nearly half a century, the most heated arguments in linguistic field are oriented around Saussure's principle of arbitrariness, indicating that the question of arbitrariness of linguistic signs turns out to be too complicated to understand, too hard to answer.

① See Fang Li's preface to *A Study on Linguistic Motivations*. The quotation is translated by the author.

The study on motivation of English lexis has a number of consequences, bother empirical and theoretical. In particular, as we will discuss at length in the following chapters, it has its most direct impact on the account of the phenomena in lexis teaching and learning.

The exploration in motivation of English lexis to a certain extent, will undoubtedly make a clarification of the relationship between the two, meanwhile, will enhance linguistic theories.

This study is also a contribution to cognitive linguistics. On one hand, the three stages of the arguments on the relationship between arbitrariness and motivation give us a cognitive explanation to the Saussure's philosophy of linguistics. On the other hand, the occurance of the term "motivation" marks the gradual developing process of human's cognition in language's nature and thinking patterns (方立, 2001). [①] indicating there is a cognitive route in the history of linguistic study. Motivation study attempts to achieve the good.

1.3 Definition of Motivation

When asked why parents take one name instead of another for their child, sometimes they give a definite reason, such as the name conveys best wishes, stands for a memorable event, or symbolizes something meaningful. However, parents sometimes choose a name, but cannot give any specific reason for doing so. They take the name, most likely, because they are following others, or because the name itself sounds pleasant and/or fashionable. The desire to follow others, the requirement to pursue a pleasant sound, or the need to be fashionable is

① See Fang Li's preface to《语言理据研究》。The English lines quoted here were translated by the author.

the motivation of the name.

Motivation is the subdivision of the study of the principle of arbitrariness proposed by Saussure, which refers to the essential relationship(s) between the signifier (which carries meaning) and the signified (the meaning which is carried) (Saussure, 2001). Although the study of motivations can be traced back to very early time, it is, however, the release of Saussure's Course in General Linguistics that really evoked a heated argument on the issue. Initially, the issue was proposed against Saussure's principle of arbitrariness. As a result, linguistic signs have once been considered either arbitrary or motivated, or both. Some even believe parts of linguistic signs are arbitrary, while parts motivated. This study has no attempts to argue about the relationship of the two. It is the issue of motivation that inspires the author to study further.

What is motivation? Apart from Saussure's explanation, interpretations of motivation vary from individual to individual. According to *Longman Dictionary of Language Teaching & Applied Linguistics*, motivation in general refers to "the driving force in any situation that leads to action" (Richards et al, 2003: 343). It suits language acquisition but not linguistic signs. According to Yan Chen-song (2000), motivations in language indicate various relationships between the signifier and the signified, or those among signifiers. They reveal the meaning of the forms or point to the connections among the forms. Yan's definition tallies with Saussure's. Wang Ai-lu et al (2002) define it as "anything that motivates or inspires a linguistic sign to appear, to change, and to develop"①. As to the definitions above, we

① It is translated by the author.

would like to make a clarification. First, the signifier and the signified are related, directly or indirectly. Second, a linguistic sign is an entity that carries the phonological, morphological and semantic form of the signifier. The driving force that leads the appearance of any linguistic signs is the motivation. With the new definition in mind, we would like to make a new classification of motivations of linguistic signs, hence giving a detailed description of the conceptual characteristics of them.

1.4　Classification of Motivation

With regard to the motivations, different scholars have different classifications. Ulmann, who firstly investigates motivation attentively, categorizes motivations into three types: phonetic motivations, morphological motivations and semantic motivations (1962: 84-92, 205-206), which constitute the internal system of linguistic signs illustrated in Figure 1-1.

motivations { phonological motivations / morphological motivations / semantic motivations }

Figure 1-1　Ulmann's classification

Now that motivation is defined as the driving force that leads the appearance of any linguistic signs, it is certainly related to the outside world. Luckily, Yan Chen-song classifies motivations into two main types, the external motivations and internal motivations. The former implies that linguistic signs are related to the outside referents. It contains onomatopoeia, pictographic, iconicity and economic motivations. The latter deals with linguistic signs themselves including phonetic, morphological and semantic motivations(2000: 1-6)(see Figure 1-2).

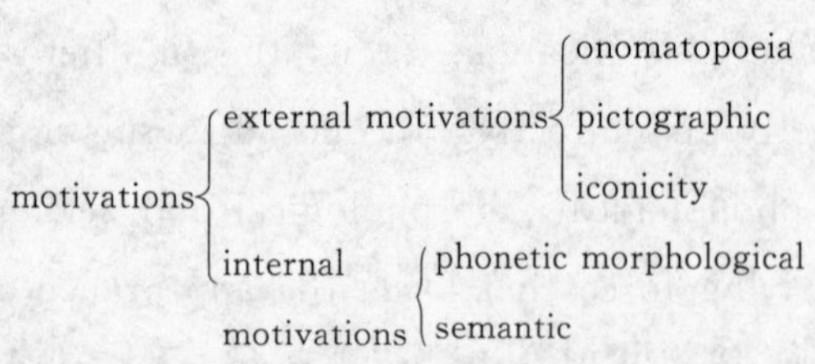

Figure 1-2 Yan Chen-song's classification

Yan's classification directs motivation study from linguistic signs themselves to the related outside world. Unfortunately, Yan's classification partly confuses the internal motivation and external motivation by categorizing both onomatopoeia and pictographic to external motivations. We would rather classify motivations into two main types: the internal motivations and external motivations. The former deals with linguistic signs themselves including phonetic, morphological and semantic motivations, while the latter extends to a various fields, like cognition, psychology, etymology, biology, etc. (see Figure 1-3).

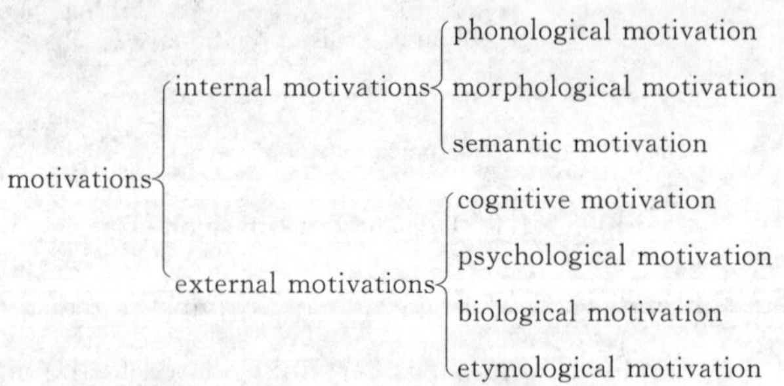

Figure 1-3 Our classification

1.5 Conceptual Characteristics of Motivation

When exploring motivations of linguistic signs, we interestingly find that motivations can be investigated either from the signs themselves, or from the outside world around them. A linguistic sign might be the direct product of the motivation. In other word, it is the motivation that directly motivates the occurence of certain linguistic sign. Motivations in this sense are linear, illustrated in Figure 1-4:

linguistic sign ----------------▸ motivation

Figure 1-4 Linear features of lexical motivations

Let's take *Watergate* for example. Originally, *Watergate*, referred to the Watergate Hotel in Washington, D. C., and is now a political scandal involving abuse of power, bribery and obstruction of justice. Reasons can be traced back to the US Presidential Election in 1972. Before the Election, in order to stand a dominating position in election to the Democratic Party, National Committee officials attempted to install bugging devices in the telephones of Democrats. With the scandal exposed to light, Nixon became the first president in American history to resign from office. From then on, *Watergate Affair* became a general term used to describe a complex web of political scandals, and motivates a new meaning of the word *Watergate*. The motivation of *Watergate* in this sense is linear.

Motivation might also be pyramid-shaped, implying that a set of family linguistic signs share the same motivation, as illustrated in Figure 1-5:

The letters S on the bottom stand for linguistic signs.

Let's come back to the word *Watergate* again. As a political

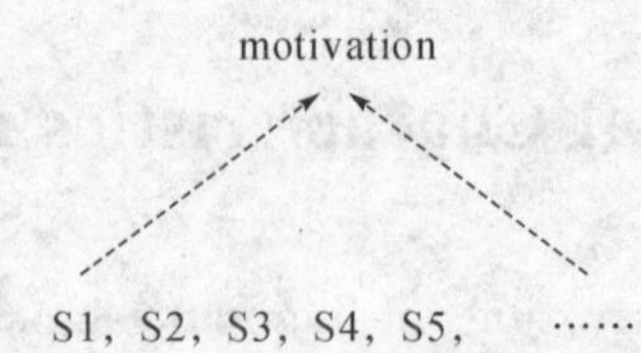

Figure 1-5 Pyramid-shaped motivations

scandal, the *Watergate Affair* caused a great stir in the world for a long period. Greatly affected in language, the synonyms with the suffix *-gate* kept dramatically increasing in number. For example, the event that an oil company in England sold oil to racialists in North Africa was called *Oilgate*. The story of how South Africa's ruling party "offered solidarity" to then Iraq leader Saddam Hussein in exchange for crude oil and how State resources were used to help the party in this project was known as *Oilgate*. The case that one of the chemical companies located in Michigan, USA, once mixed poisons with feed additives, which poisoned many cattle was called *Cattlegate*. The affair that the USA former president Jimmy Carter's brother, Billy Carter, once accepted payment for goods to commit illegal affairs was called *Billygate*. The incident that top operatives in Ronald Reagan's presidential campaign helped Reagan for a crucial debate with Carter by making the most of the illegally obtained papers, and won a thoroughbred performance was labeled *debategate*. The Iran-Contra Affair was known as *Irangate*, in which President Ronald Reagan's administration sold arms to Iran, an avowed enemy. Years ago, when the sexual scandal about Clinton and Lewinsky was known as *zippergate*. From the new dictionary of English neologisms, we could find more words with *-gate* as *Briefing-gate*, *cookiegate*, *Contragate*, *copygate*, *gibberishgate*, *Godsgate*, *Gospelgate*, *Guinnessgate*, *harborgate*, *Heavengate*, *Inkathagage*, *Keelgate*, *Koreagate*, *Pageantgate*, *Pearlgate*, *pseudo-gate*,

Reagangate, *salvationgate*, *Sewergate*, *Sharongate*, *Stargate*, *sugargate*, *targate*, *Totegate*, *Walk-on-gate*, etc.

In fact, after the *Watergate Affair*, new words with the suffix-*gate*, bearing the implication of "scandals", occured one after another not only in English vocabulary, but also in other languages. We can safely conclude that *-gate* has already been an actual suffix in word building. Words built in this way are motivated. The motivation is pyramid-shaped, implying that a group of family linguistic signs as mentioned above share the same motivation.

The fact that we normally have a choice between categories on different levels of generality, indicates the arbitrariness of linguistic signs. The fact that we may have a choice only between categories on different levels of generality instead of on other levels indicates that linguistic signs are motivated.

When reviewing some related publications, we find that some study the motivations of linguistic signs from the cognitive perspective, called cognitive motivations, while others in the biographic angle, called biographic motivation. Motivations can be explored philosophically, etymologically, and even physically. They are not within but beyond the linguistic signs, and closely related to the outside world. In this sense, we say motivations are divergent, as illustrated in Figure 1-6.

In Figure 1-6, the letters *M* stand for different motivations from different perspectives. In this sense, motivations tend to involve more and more domains, being more and more open. Each perspective constitutes a good issue over motivations. The case that motivations of linguistic signs extend so far exhibits the divergent characteristics of motivation of linguistic signs.

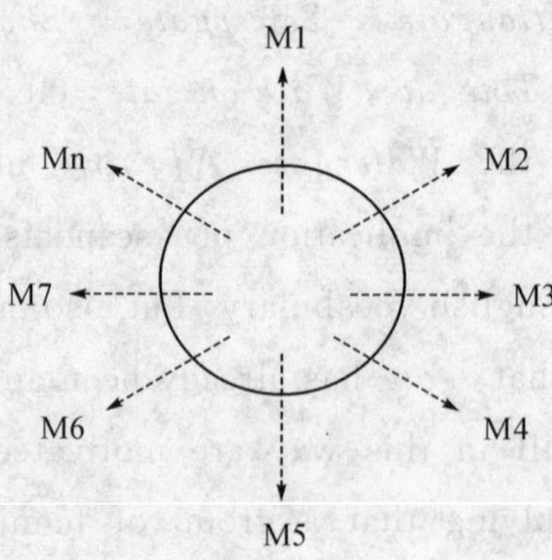

Figure 1-6 Aspects of motivation

1.6 Theoretical Framework of This Study

To sum up, motivation refers to the driving force that leads to the appearance of any linguistic signs. Motivations can be studied not only within linguistic signs themselves, that is, the internal motivations, but also from the outside world, that is, the external motivations. Phonological motivations, morphological motivations and semantic motivations constitute the internal motivations of linguistic signs. The different perspectives, from which we study motivations including cognitive motivations, etymological motivations, psychological motivations, etc., constitute the external motivations of linguistic signs. The linearity, pyramid, and divergence constitute the three characteristics of motivation. All above constitutes a theoretical framework of this study.

The study on motivations of linguistic signs is not only an extension of Saussure's principle of arbitrariness, but also an attempt to investigate Saussure's theory on general linguistics.

Chapter Two Motivation, Arbitrariness and Iconicity

There are two main issues running through this study, one is the concepts of arbitrariness and motivation of linguistic signs; the other is a review of the arguments over the arbitrariness and motivation. A better understanding of the two terms helps to clarify the relationship between arbitrariness and motivation of linguistic signs, serving to guide the study of the relationship of the two to a non-biased direction. What is likely to be ignored is that the arguments over arbitrariness and motivation reflect man's cognitive process. In this sense, cognitive linguistics is another theoretical basis of this study.

2.1 Arbitrariness and Motivation

2.1.1 Conceptual Connotation of Arbitrariness and Motivation

Now that motivation is defined as the driving force in any situation that leads to the appearance of linguistic signs, the pair term arbitrariness seems easier to understand. It seems not to be the case, however. It is well known that Saussure puts the principle of arbitrariness in first place in the list of the various principles. This is because there is no "natural tie" between a signifying expression (signifiant) and a signified content (signifié). Since "the link between signal and signification is arbitrary" and thus "the linguistic sign is arbitrary"(Saussure, 2001:67).

However, he also points out that "the word *arbitrary* also calls for comment. It must not be taken that a signal depends on the free choice of the speaker" (ibid, 68). This means linguistic sign is relatively arbitrary. In other words, it is motivation-orientedly arbitrary, or arbitrary on a motivated basis. However, the different interpretations to the principle of arbitrariness lead to an half-century argument.

2.1.2 Relationship between Arbitrariness and Motivation

Although the study over the relationship between arbitrariness and motivation can be traced back to very early time, it is, however, the release of Saussure's Course in General Linguistics that evoked a heated argument. To fully understand the principle of arbitrariness, it is perhaps better to review the development of the various arguments over this issue. As to the relationship over arbitrariness and motivation in language study, opinions vary among scholars in different times, which can be concluded as follows: either-arbitrary-or-motivated viewpoint, some-arbitrary-while-others-motivated viewpoint, and both-arbitrary-and-motivated viewpoint.

2.1.2.1 Either Arbitrary or Motivated

The principle of arbitrariness proposed by Saussure has been argued for nearly half a century. Regardless of Saussure's own explanation, this principle has evoked various understandings and explanations of the nature or natures of linguistic signs. Some scholars point out that

Saussure's core insight lies at the heart of deconstruction and a host of related intellectual fashions. They say since he defines a linguistic sign as the combination of a signifier and a signified, that the signifier (which carries meaning) and the signified (the meaning which is carried) have no essential relationship, thus the lack of relationship exposes the arbitrary nature of all languages and language-like systems. The principle of arbitrariness is supported by Hockett (1960), who regards arbitrariness as the basic principle of linguistic signs; by Lyons (1977), who claims that there are sixteen natures of linguistic signs, among which arbitrariness occupies the dominant position; by Culler (1976), who suggests "both signifier and signified are purely relational or differential entities"; by Barthes; by Suo Zhenyu (索振羽, 1995), who believes that "Saussure's principle of arbitrariness is reasonable"; by Wang De-chun (王德春, 2001) and Guo Hong (郭宏, 2001) who completely or partly agree on the point that linguistic signs are arbitrarily connected with the entities, etc. The principle of arbitrariness was once in a predominant position particularly before 1980s until further study is conducted.

With a deeper insight into the natures of languages, linguistic experts have found evidence against the arbitrary nature of languages, which has led them to propose diverse opinions. The most influential representative of supporters is Holdcroft (1991), who holds the view that the arbitrariness of linguistic sign is "a questionable idea". Halliday (1985), who also questions the arbitrariness of languages, regards arbitrariness as a conflicting concept to functional linguistics. According to Pierce, motivated natures of linguistic signs may find expressions in

iconicity[①]. According to Wittgenstein, motivated natures of linguistic signs may find expressions in family resemblance[②]. Other scholars, such as Wright (1976) and Nöth (1990: 244), propose different viewpoints against arbitrariness from various perspectives. Bolinger et al(1981:11), points out that nothing related to language is arbitrary, for any element in language has its non-arbitrary sources. For years, many Chinese scholars study semiotic theories in great detail. Xu Guo-zhang (许国璋, 1991:21-22) argues that "since language belongs to a rational behavior, how is it possible to be arbitrary?". Li Bao-jia(李葆嘉,1994) holds that the relationship between the system of linguistic signs and the objective physical world (including mental world) is never arbitrary. Although opinions vary from individual to individual, they have something in common, that is, arbitrariness and motivation are considered as two conflicting concepts, indicating that linguistic signs are either arbitrary or motivated.

Even when more and more linguistic signs serve as evidence to support the motivation, the two conflicting concepts are confined to the viewpoint that those linguistic signs that are arbitrary are not motivated, or those that are motivated are not arbitrary.

2.1.2.2 Some Motivated, While Others Arbitrary

In *Course in General Linguistics*, Saussure(2001) points out two concepts: absolute arbitrariness and relative arbitrariness, explaining that "the fundamental principle of the arbitrary nature of the linguistic sign does not prevent us from distinguishing in any language between what is intrinsically arbitrary—that is, unmotivated—and what is only relatively arbitrary. (ibid,130) He cites the French words *vingt* (twenty)

① http://www.arthist.lu.se/kultsem/encyclo/iconicity.html

② http://plato.stanford.edu/entries/wittgenstein/#Lan

and *dix-neuf* (nineteen) as examples, showing *vingt* is unmotivated, whereas *dix-neuf* not unmotivated to the same extent. For *dix-neuf* evokes the words of which it is composed, *dix*(ten) and *neuf*(nine), and those of the same numerical series: *dix*(ten), *neuf*(nine), *vingt-neuf*(twenty nine), *dix-huit* (eighteen), *soixante-dix*(seventy), etc. Taken individually, *dix* and *neuf* are on the same footing as *vingt*, but *dix-neuf* is an example of relative motivation. (ibid,130) It is the samples above that lead to the belief that some linguistic signs are motivated while others are arbitrary. That is, linguistic signs can be classified into two major categories: the motivated one and the arbitrary one.

Xu Guo-zhang (许国璋,1991) (from 张绍杰, 2004: 10) once argues that linguistic signs seem arbitrary to a beginner, but motivated when he learns more, impling that whether linguistic signs are arbitrary or motivated depends on one's cognition. Suo Zhen-yu (索振羽, 1995) believes that the roots are arbitrary while derivates are motivated. Suo proceeds that the elements that constitute the relatively motivated linguistic signs (derivates and compounds) remain unmotivated. Although Wang Ai-lu et al(王艾录等, 2002: 33), hold the belief that linguistic signs are motivated, they find that scholars since Saussure are in a habit of exemplifying compounds as evidence of motivation, and simple words as evidence of arbitrariness, with the implication that the formers are motivated while the latters seem arbitrary. Zhu Yong-sheng (朱永生, 2002: 2), holds that there does exist iconicity in compounds, derivates, and in syntax. But when it comes to simple words, arbitrariness remains an unquestionable principle. Wang Rong-pei et al (汪榕培等, 1997: 98) argue that there is no natural tie between the meaning and the form of a word, both of which are conventional. However, not all of the words are absolutely conventional instead of

being unmotivated. At least some transparent words are to some degree motivated. Although the motivated words are in the minority, the knowledge of their motivations helps to understand them.

2. 1. 2. 3 Both Motivated and Arbitrary

With regard to the either-arbitrary-or-motivated viewpoint, or the some-motivated-while-others-arbitrary viewpoint, we tend to believe the key point is the different understanding of "motivation". When "motivation" is interpreted as a perceptual concept, these two viewpoints come into immergence. What differentiates one from the other is the different perspective they take. The reason why some people believe that some English words are not motivated is that when the meaning of a word semantically extends too far, the initial motivation can hardly be associated with the present word. In this sense, parts of the motivations in words are missing, which evokes an impression that linguistic signs are arbitrary.

It is not the case, however, since linguistic signs may be totally arbitrary to those who do not know it, yet are motivated to those who do, which illustrates that motivation and arbitrariness are both natures of linguistic signs. They are different concepts with absolute conflicting meanings, yet each standing as part of the features. This viewpoint guides the arguments to the third stage, and is supported by Zhang Shao-jie(张绍杰), Zhang Feng et al(张凤等), Lu Bing-fu(陆丙甫), etc.

Jespersen(1922) holds that semiotic elements do not necessarily deny the relationship between meanings and forms of words(from 申小龙, 2005: 315-316), indicating a challenge to the principle of arbitrariness.

Wang Yin (王寅,2002: 4) argues that the acceptance of iconicity does not necessarily deny arbitrariness. The new viewpoints direct the study on the arbitrariness and motivation of linguistic signs on a double-layered basis. That is, linguistic signs share both arbitrariness and motivation. Wang Ai-lu et al,(王艾录等,2002: 32) proclaim that simple signs, as well as compound signs, are motivated. They (ibid, 54-55) propose a new point that "linguistic signs are not only governed by the principle of arbitrariness but also controlled by that of motivation, the two principles being both in conflict with each other and meanwhile in agreement with each other, which constitute the most essential principles of language".

As a new achievement in this field, the publication *A Study in Arbitrariness of Linguistic signs: Exploring Saussure's Philosophy of Linguistics*(张绍杰, 2004), reveals the two natures in greater detail. Zhang points out that the distinction between absolute arbitrariness and relative arbitrariness proposed by Saussure enables us to see that the notion of arbitrariness can only be explained in different layers, though Saussure didn't make any declaration (2004: 5). Zhang holds that in Saussure's linguistics, both arbitrariness and motivation are not in conflict with each other, but in agreement with each other, which constitute a unity of opposites. On one hand, language system provides a prerequisite to the free relationship between the signifier and the signified. On the other hand, the system restricts the degree of its arbitrariness, that is, it determines how the signifier and signified are organized. In a word, language as a system remains a balance, with arbitrariness and motivation depending on each other, interacting with each other in the process of its development (2004).

Pei Wen(裴文,2003: 207), who supports Saussure's arbitrariness, believes that on the one hand, as a fundamental principle, the principle of arbitrariness ranks the first, motivation the second; on the other hand, they are both natures of linguistic signs, each having different extents, and categories. It is neither acceptable to deny one by stressing the other, nor reasonable to oppose one by hiding the other.

Zhao Yan-fang (赵艳芳, 2001: 35) argues that, cognitively speaking, words are somewhat arbitrary in a basic-level category, but are motivated in the process of word-formation in which more words in a subordinate category, a superordinate category, or in larger linguistic units (like phrases, sentences) are formed.

Zhang Feng et al (张风等, 2005: 16) find that the viewpoint of iconicity proposed by functional linguists (including cognitive linguistics) is not against Saussure's arbitrariness, for those who support arbitrariness or iconicity are yet to reach an agreement on some key concepts (including arbitrariness, iconicity and motivation). They hold that when taken individually, linguistic signs are arbitrary or unmotivated, yet when taken as a unity, they are relatively motivated (2005: 17).

Lu Bing-fu et al (陆丙甫等, 2005) argue that all linguistic symbols (signs) and their combinations are motivated by whatever causes, and the overstatement of language arbitrariness could be ascribed to the loss of causal traces and complex mutual interactions between different motivations. We find that, linguistically speaking, among synonymous paradigms, the superordinate of the hyponyms in a certain paradigm is motivated, while the hyponyms are superordinate-orientedly arbitrary in each group. Semantically speaking, synonyms are arbitrary, but not arbitrary if their semantic connotations are considered. In other words, the prototype concepts are usually more motivated, while primary ones are more arbitrary. Fussy terms are more motivated while precise ones are more arbitrary. As to the part-whole relations, the whole is more motivated, with the part being more arbitrary.

2.1.3 Summary

In the preceding pages, we introduced the notion of Saussure's principle of arbitrariness, suggesting that the process of the gradual understanding of Saussure's principle reflects the cognitive process of human beings.

When Saussure discovered the natures of linguistic signs, he conceptualized them with arbitrariness and motivation. In *Course in General Linguistics*, Saussure regards the principle of arbitrariness as "the first principle" of linguistic signs, hence provoking a heated argument over the nature or natures of linguistic signs. Although some linguists such as Suo Zhen-yu (索振宇), Wang De-chun(王德春), Guo Hong(郭宏), completely or partly agree on the point that linguistic signs are arbitrarily connected with the entities, some like Xu Guo-zhang(许国璋), Hu Zhuang-lin(胡壮麟), Zhang Shao-jie(张绍杰), Wang Yin(王寅), Wang Ai-li(王艾录), Si Fu-zhen(司富珍) once question it[①], and some even develop Saussure's theory by studying linguistic signs in more perspectives. The fact that more and more linguists begin to view the relationship between arbitrariness and motivation on a layer-to-layered basis indicates a cognitive progress in linguistic study. The transition from the belief that arbitrariness occupies a dominant position (see Culler, 1976; Barthes, 1977; Lyons, 1991; etc.) to the questioning of the principle of arbitrariness, (Holdcroft, 1991; Halliday, 1978; Pierce, 1985; Wittgenstein, 1953) and then to the different viewpoints against arbitrariness (see Wright, 1976; Nöth, 1990; 李葆嘉, 1994) marked a cognitive route of motivation study, along which we may conduct our study, with the help of the findings on it, coming with more achievements on language study.

---

① The quotation comes out according to *On Arbitrariness and Cognition of Linguistic Signs*(朱永生, 2002).

2.2 Our Opinion

So far we have spoken of the relationship between arbitrariness and motivation, and introduced the notion of motivations in lexis. The former may guide us in the study on motivations of words on a non-biased direction. The latter helps us to better understand the concept of motivation. Initially, the term *motivation* was discussed together with arbitrariness. Later, the two issues are respectively under exploration. We hold that linguistic sign, in itself, including words, has its own motivations. However, the motivations make sense only to a certain extent; in other words, motivations of words are only a question of "degree", but not an "either-or" question. The reason why we could not explain the appearance of parts of the language phenomenon or words, and of their motivations, is that it is beyond man's cognition. The world is full of mysteries. When a volcano broke out in an earlier time, man used to believe that it was the result of a monster losing its temper, but with the development of science and technology, and with man's increased knowledge about nature, more reasonable explanations are given. A volcano erupting is a natural phenomenon, while language is a semiotic system that reflects the natural world. Motivations in words are not necessarily a direct product of a real world, but cognition of it. Until recently, we could hardly find all the motivations in every linguistic sign, simply because it is beyond man's cognition. With the increased development and research in cognitive linguistics, more and more motivations will be exposed.

In the process of this study, we find that arbitrariness and motivation belong to two different concepts in different levels, not in conflict with each other, but in agreement with each other. Linguistically speaking, among synonymous paradigms, the superordinate of the hyponyms in a certain paradigm is motivated, while the hyponyms are superordinate-orientedly arbitrary in each group. Semantically speaking, synonyms are arbitrary, but not arbitrary if their semantic connotations are considered. In other words, the prototype concepts are usually more motivated, while primary ones are more arbitrary. Fussy terms are more motivated while precise ones are more arbitrary. As to the part-whole relations, the whole is more motivational, with the part being more arbitrary. Cognitively speaking, words are somewhat arbitrary in a basic-level category, but are motivated in the word-formation process in which more words in a subordinate category, a superordinate category, or in larger linguistic units (like phrases, sentences) are formed (赵艳芳, 2001: 35).

This study serves as a trigger to the further studies on more extensive related issues. Interests in any related issues aroused by this study will ensure more and more academic achievements. In fact, some researching projects revolving around motivation study have been approved and are being conducted. We are willing to devote the rest of our lives to language researches and language teaching.

Chapter Three Phonological Motivations of English Lexis

According to the categories of lexical motivations we made, phonological motivations entail four main parts: onomatopoeia, phonaestheme, reduplication and phonological change. (see Figure 3-1)

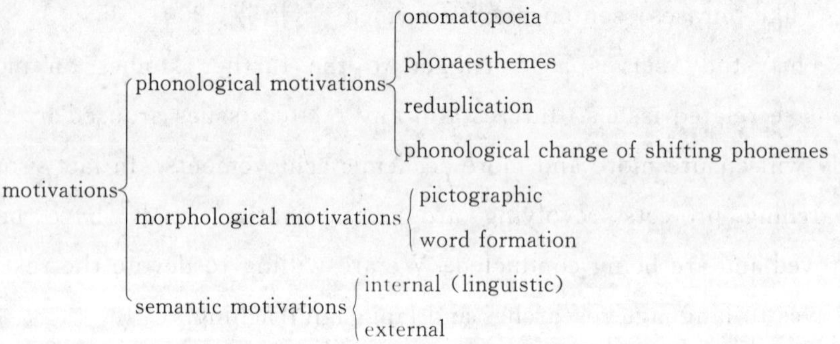

Figure 3-1 Types and subtypes of lexical motivations

Although phonological motivations are not what we intends to focus on in this study, it is our responsibility to present a brief introduction here, for phonetics is one of the three components of lexis.

If we say words can be phonologically motivated, we mean there must be some similarities between the phonology of words and the sound in the natural world, or there must be some relationship between the sound and the word. Phonological motivations generally involves onomatopoeic, phonaesthemes, reduplication of certain syllables, phonological shifting and change of phonemes occurred.

3.1 Onomatopoeia Motivation

Onomatopoeia, or echoism is a combination of sounds in a word that imitates or suggests what the word refers to. The onomatopoeia motivation lies in the similarity between a word and the objective world.

Naturalists believe that the origin of language lies in onomatopoeia. They think people began talking by imitating the sounds around in nature. Hence words emerged in the way of imitating represents corresponding senses.

With regard to onomatopoeia, most particular researches have been conducted. Ma Bing-yi(马秉义,2004:39-40), collected more than 400 echo words in his study, and divided them into three main categories: the echo words of animals, of natural phenomena, and of crashing and collision. But we prefer to divide them into the other three categories: the echo words from human beings, from animals, and from non-animals.

Firstly, when human beings feel happy, they may *laugh*, *chortle*, *chuckle*, *giggle*, *guffaw*, *snicker*, *sniggle*, and *hee-haw*. When sad, they may *cry*, *sob*, *wail*, *weep*, *sniff*, *snivel*, *whimper*, *whine*, *moan*, *bawl*, and *howl*. If they want to be loud enough, they may *shout*, *whoop*, *yell*, *howl*, *scream*, *shriek*, *bawl*, and *roar*. On the contrary, they may *murmur*, *mutter*, *mumble*, *grunt*, *whisper*, *buzz*, *drone*, *hum*, *purr* and *brool*.

As for the echo words from some animals, we could hear the *crunch* of a bear, the *buzzing* of bees. We could see the fish *flopping* about on

the bank, snakes *hissing* when getting angry. A rooster usually *crows* at daybreak, while a hen keeps *cackling* after she lays an egg. Moreover, ducks *quack*, goats *bleat*, cows *moo*, pigeons *coo*, crickets *chirp*, pigs *grunt*, frogs *croak*, flies *hum* and *buzz*, sheep and goats *bleat*, mice *squeak*, wolves *howl*, lions *roar*, tigers *growl*, cranes *whoop*, horses *neigh*, etc. Moreover, bees *hum*, beetle *drone*, birds *twitter*, bulls *bellow*, cows *low*. Generally, cats *miaow*, *miaou*, *meow*, or *mew*. But when they are happy, they *purr*. A dog usually *barks*, but it also *howls*, *yelps*, *whines* and *growls* when it notices something unusual. Wang Feng-xin(王逢鑫, 2003: 144-147) suggests about 80 echo words of animals in his *English-Chinese Comparative Semantics*.

When it comes to the sound in the nature, a good case in point is the word *dingdong*, the sound of bells striking again and again. Also, we can say the wall falls with a *crash*, the rain falls *pitter-patter* on the window. We could hear the swords *clashing*, the whip *cracking*. At the railway station, we could hear a train *puffing* towards the town. At wedding, we *clink* our glasses together to toast the bride and groom. Before computer, we could get the information we need just by *clicking* the mouse. Also in the dark, we could *flip* on the lights.

What is mentioned above reveals that echo words did come by means of imitating sound.

Roget's Thesaurus (from 王逢鑫, 2003:149-150) classified the echo words into eight main types (let's take only verbs as examples), some of which belong to the echo words from nature.

(1) Sudden and violent sounds: *rap*, *snap*, *tap*, *knock*, *click*, *clash*, *crack*, *crash*, *pop*, *slam*, *bang*, *clap*, *thump*, *plump*, *toot*...

(2) Repeated and protracted sounds: *roll*, *drum*, *rumble*, *rattle*, *clatter*, *rustle*, *roar*, *drone*, *patter*, *clack*, *hum*, *trill*, *shake*, *chime*,

peal, *toll*, *tick*, *beat*...

(3) Resonance: *ring*, *ding*, *sing*, *jingle*, *gingle*, *chink*, *clink*, *tink*, *chine*, *gurgle*, *splash*, *guggle*, *echo*...

(4) No-resonance: *muffle*...

(5) Hissing sounds: *hiss*, *buzz*, *whiz*, *rustle*, *fizz*, *sizzle*, *swish*, *wheeze*, *whistle*, *snuffle*, *squash*, *sneeze*...

(6) Harsh sounds: *creak*, *grate*, *jar*, *burr*, *pipe*, *twang*, *jangle*, *clank*, *clink*, *scream*, *yelp*...

(7) Cry: *cry*, *roar*, *shout*, *bawl*, *brawl*, *halloo*, *hail*, *hoop*, *whoop*, *yell*, *bellow*, *howl*, *scream*, *screech*, *screak*, *shriek*, *shrill*, *squeak*, *squeal*, *squall*, *whine*, *whinny*, *pule*, *pipe*, *yaup*, *cheer*, *hurrah*, *hoot*, *grumble*, *moan*, *groan*, *snore*, *snort*, *grunt*...

By means of echo words, we may enjoy the vividness and analogy in talking or writing, thus leaving a deep impression on listeners or readers.

3.2 Phonaestheme Motivation

There are certain individual sounds, or groups of sounds, which do not represent a specific meaning but appear to be vaguely associated with some kinds of meanings. These sounds are called phonaesthemes. For example: The vowel [ʌ] is found in words associated with various kinds of dullness or indistinctness, as in *dull*, *thud*, *thunder*, *dusk*, *blunt*, *mud* and *slump*, etc.

Similarly, the sound [ʌmp] (spelled as -ump) as in *clump*, *dump*, *bump*, *lump* is often found at the final part of words which are associated with heaviness and clumsiness.

Other examples are the high front vowels [ɪ] and [iː], which

frequently occur as phonaesthemes in words associated with the state of being small or little, as in *wee*, *teeny-weeny*, *mini*, *thin* and *little*.

3.3 Reduplication Motivation

Reduplication is the formation of word by reduplicating certain morphemes or phonemes.

There are two main categories in English: rhyme motivated compounds and ablaut motivated compounds.

In Rhyme Motivated Compounds, the repetition of the bases in compounds involves copying the rhyme. Here *rhyme* means what it means in poetry: the vowels and any consonant(s) that follow it in the last syllable are identical. For example, *nitwit*, *titbit*, *teeny-weeny*, *helter-skelter*, *hobnob*.

In Ablaut Motivated Compounds, the consonants are copied while the vowels are changed. *Ablaut* means a change in the root vowel. Examples of this kind are *tip-top*, *shilly-shally*, *wibble-wobble*, *tittle-title*, *tick-tack*, *ping-pong*, *ding-dong*, *snip-snap*, *pit-a-pat*.

The meanings of the words in partial reduplication cannot be deduced easily from their component elements, and the motivation in partial reduplication exists mainly for the reason of word-formation. As mentioned above, the word-formation motivations may lie in rhythm or ablaut. So the motivations existing in these two kinds of reduplication have different features: the former concerns more about the relation between meaning and expression, while the latter concerns more about the formational motivations of these words.

3.4 Phonological Shifting Motivation

Study indicates that the meaning of a word can be deduced from both an existing word and the connection between the new-deduced one and the original one in phonological shifting.

A word can be changed into another one by the stress shifting, sometimes with the same meaning but different part of speech, sometimes with a complete change of meaning. Sometimes, the part of speech can be deduced by the shifting of stress. Sometimes, the meaning can also be deduced. For example, when the word *present* is pronounced with its initial syllable stressed, it is a noun meaning *gift*, while when its second syllable stressed, it is a verb meaning *to give*, *to offer* or *to submit*. More examples of this kind are as follows:

Table 3-1 Phonological motivation by stress shifting

Noun	Verb
'excuse	ex'cuse
'comfort	com'fort
'increase	in'crease
'subject	sub'ject
'contract	con'tract
'desert	de'sert
'digest	di'gest

The shifting of stress also occur in the derivational process as in *Canada*, a noun when the first syllable is stressed, and in *Canadian*, a noun or an adjective when the second syllable is stressed. Further examples are as follows:

Table 3-2 Phonological shifting motivation in derivational process

'China *n.*	Chi'nese *n.* & *adj.*
'Italy *n.*	I'talian *n.* & *adj.*
'Europe *n.*	Euro'pean *n.* & *adj.*
'preference *n.*	pre'fer *v.*
presen'tation *n.*	pre'sent *v.*
moti'vation *n.*	'motive *n.*
for'mation *n.*	form *v.* & *n.*
popu'larity *n.*	'popular *adj.*
pro'gressive *adj.*	'progress *v.* & *n.*

The deeper motivations of phonological shifting deserves further study.

3.5 The Change of Phonemes Motivation

In English there are some words with the same orthographic form but different pronunciation, different meaning or different part of speech. For example, the word *use* is a noun when pronounced as [juːs], but when pronounced as [juːz], it is a verb. More examples are as follows: The word *close* is a verb when pronounced as [kləʊz], but a noun when pronounced as [kləʊs].

Now we come to a conclusion that a change in pronunciation of a consonant or a vowel often occur together with the shifting of the stress and the change of the meaning. The change of consonants may just affect the part of speech of a word with the basic meaning unchanged, or it may produce two words with totally different meanings.

3.6 Summary

Phonological motivations, which studies the relationship between a word and the objective world, is generally considered as the most traditional kind of motivations. Among the four, onomatopoeia can be most highly motivated. The probable reason is because there is direct relationship between onomatopoeia and the objective world.

Many scholars tend to believe that not all the words' meanings formed phonologically can be deduced. Yet, we tend to believe that any sound as well as any word can be both motivated and arbitrary on a layer-to-layer basis. By saying onomatopoeia can be the most highly motivated, we mean the motivation in onomatopoeia is the easiest to be traced upon. In other words, it is on the surface so that it is most apparent. In other words, we may find phonological motivations in the onomatopoeia *miaow*, indicating the sound of a cat can be phonologically motivated. Yet either *miaow*, *miaou*, *meow* or *mew* can be used arbitrarily to indicate the sound of a cat. The motivation of the onomatopoeia of *miaow* restricts *miaow*, *miaou*, *meow* or *mew* in a relatively arbitrary scope.

Chapter Four Morphological Motivations of New English Lexis

Lexical morphology studies the internal structure of words, and the rules by which words are formed (胡壮麟, 2001: 84). In this section, we intend to focus on the topic from two main perspectives: the pictographic perspective and the word-formation perspective.

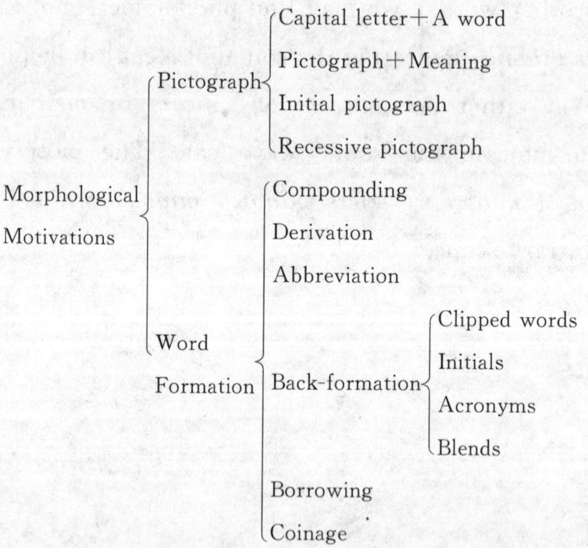

Figure 4-1 Classification and morphological motivations by Hu Zhuang-lin

4.1 Pictographic Motivation

Studies on the pictographic motivations in new English lexis are mainly conducted by Chinese linguists, which is probably because Chinese words are pictographic. Zhang Ke-ding (张克定, 2001) cites the word *mouse* as an example to support his viewpoint that the derived meaning of a linguistic sign can be pictographically motivated. He concludes that since *mouse* (a small animal that is covered in fur and has a long thin tail)① and the *mouse* (a small device that is moved by hand across a surface to control the movement of the cursor on a computer screen)② when attached to the computer, share similarities in shape, which contributes to an association to each other. Therefore, a new meaning of *mouse* was derived from its original one. Yuan Li (袁立, 2000) gives a vivid description of English words based on the six categories of Chinese characters. He states that at least three English words—*eye*, *bed*, and *broom*, possess pictographic characteristics. Based on this theory, the word *eye* looks as if two eyes are fixed along the two sides of a nose, the word *bed* looks like a real bed, and the word *broom* is a combination of *b* and *room*, with the letter *b* shaped like a broom for cleaning a room. Therefore, he theorizes that English words possess pictographic characteristics. Yue De-yu (岳德宇, 2003) writes a book named *An Efficient Technique to Learn 4,000 English Words* by making full use of the Chinese word-formation characteristics. The release of the publication caused a great stir in the book market, as the writer's fresh viewpoint challenges the traditional English learning

① http://reader.skybig.net/english2english_dics.php? letter=mouse

② http://reader.skybig.net/english2english_dics.php? letter=mouse

habits. Although his point remains controversial, the fact that 50,000 books were ordered in January of 2003 amazes the academic field.

4.1.1 Pictographic Capital Letter and a Word

The first category includes the expressions with a pictographic capital letter and the word itself. Examples are as follows: A-tent, T-shirt, V-belt, X-axis, S-hook, U-turn, V-sign, Y-front.

4.1.2 The Mixture of Pictograph and Meaning

The following words are a mixture of its form and meaning.

rainbow	rain + bow
honeycomb	honey + comb
paperbag	paper + bag

4.1.3 Initial Pictographs

Yuan (2000) also points out that in some English words, certain letters symbolize certain meanings according to their appearance. For example:

cap	c+ap
mount	m+ount
orb	o+rb
orbit	o+rbit
oval	o+val
oven	o+ven

4.1.4 Recessive Pictographs

Sometimes the initial letters of English words possess certain natures of the pictographic figures. In the following words, the letter *s* is shaped like a snake and is pronounced as [s].

snake	s+nake
serpent	s+erpent

Letters "sl" at the initial part of English words, implies the tendency to slide. Words alike are:

slick	s+lick
slide	s+lide
sled	s+led
slip	s+lip

Verbs started with "tr" usually refer to moving by foot, i.e., *trace*, *track*, *tramp*, *trample*, *travel*, *trudge*, etc.

Pictographic characteristics of English letters and words meet more challenges, more controversies, and even more criticism. Some argue that they may immediately refute the point by presenting inverse samples (户进菊)[①]. In our eyes, pictographic motivations are at least one of the features of English words. To say *s* symbolizes a snake does not necessarily deny the fact that it can also symbolize something else, therefore, we can say pictographic motivation is one of the morphological motivations in new English lexis.

4.2 Word-formation Motivation

Some linguists agree that affixation, compounding and conversion are the three major processes of word-formation, while the minor processes include clipping, acronym, blending, back-formation, reduplication, words from proper names, neoclassical formation and

① Having read my thesis, Dr. Hu argued with me over this point by telephone.

miscellaneous (杨良生, 1991). Apart from the three major processes, some linguists catalogue the left into affixing, abbreviating, and back-forming (李冰梅, 2005). For the convenience of this study, we would classify them into compounding, derivation, abbreviation, back-formation, borrowing, and coinage, with clipping, initials, acronyms and blending being different forms of abbreviation. This study will primarily probe into the methods in word compounding, derivation, and abbreviation.

4.2.1 Motivations in Compounding

Lexically, compounding is a "word+word" formation. It is a unit consisting of two or more stems (or bases), which can be nouns, adjectives, and verbs, composed of two or more words or parts of words (written as one or more words, or joined by a hyphen), but the bulk of them are adjectives and nouns. For example, *bungee jumping*, *mouse potato*, *air pollution*, and *business-woman*. It can be quite lengthy, for example, *the jumping-on-a-chair-at-the-sight-of-a-mouse era*.

For English, compounding is perhaps the most powerful word-building process, which is represented by the following examples:

home theatre: television and video equipment designed to reproduce the experience of being in a movie theater at home.

home cinema: an elaborate home set-up of electronics for the viewing of movies as one would at the cinema, often with big screens and surround-sound stereo; also called home theater.

home boy: (1) (with a possessive) a fellow member of an American-style gang of youths;

(2) any member of such a gang.

call bird: a bird taught to allure others into a snare.

call boy: (1) A boy who calls the actors in a theater; a boy who transmits the orders of the captain of a vessel to the engineer, helmsman, etc.

(2) A waiting boy who answers a call, or comes at the ringing of a bell; a bell boy.

call note: the note naturally used by the male bird to call the female.

call girl: a female prostitute who can be hired by telephone

street girl: a prostitute who attracts customers by walking the streets

(From Online English Dictionary[①])

4.2.2 Motivations in Derivation

Derivation mainly refers to the word formation by using affixes, which usually consists of "familiar words + new elements". For example, *Reaganism* (1966) refers to the policies and principles advocated by Ronald Reagan. This term particularly embraces his free-market, low-tax economic policies, and his hard-line anti-Communist foreign policy. In 1976, the word *Reaganite* was first coined, followed by *Reaganomics*, *Reaganaut*, *Reagan democrat*, *Reaganize*, etc.

Generally speaking, derivatives are formed with roots and affixes, but during the process, slight changes often occur to meet the needs of pronunciation. The meanings of the derivative are mainly determined by its root. The meanings of affixes are comparatively fixed and the rules of forming derivatives are usually analyzable, allowing that derivatives have

① http://dictionary.reference.com

a high level of motivations.

In the process of new word formation, we usually take advantage of a word or part of it, which might represent an event or something to coin a new word by combining it with another. The word *Marathon* was originally the name of a place in Greece. The word was first used in a story about a soldier in the Marathon battle who ran to report the victory to Greece and then died. The long-distance foot race has become one of the sporting events of the Olympic Games since that time. Later, its meaning extended, with the implication of a long contest or event requiring great endurance. Still later, people began to create new words by combining the suffix *-thon* with other words, with the meaning of boring and endless activities, like *talkathon*, *walkathon*, *telethon*, *swimathon*, *preachathon*, *bike-athon*, *skate-athon*, *aquathon*, etc. Recently, words with -(*a*) *thon* are great in number, as *cut-a-thon*, *dance-a-thon*, *jog-a-thon*, *phone-a-thon*, *pledge-a-thon*, *swap-a-thon*, *litterathon*, *novel-athon*, *awake-a-thon*, etc. Even *read-athon*, and *poethon* are widely discussed in schools today.

In modern English, affixes are more and more commonly used. As a result, new words formed in this way keep increasing and can be highly motivated. The reasons for this phenomenon will be analyzed in the following part of this study. Here, let's pay special attention to a new word-formation phenomenon, when leaving out, adding or changing some letters, so that some words may switch into affixes. For example, one of the meanings of "alcoholic" is "relating to, or caused by alcohol". (Chambers, 1998:25) Since 1970s, new words with affix *-oholic* have been in great number, with their meanings slightly changed.

sleepaholic	a person who sleeps too much

workaholic	a person whose primary interest is work
chocoholic	a person who likes chocolates very much
mariholic	a person who is addicted to smoking marijuana
sexaholic	a person who has excessive sex desire
filmholic	a person who likes films very much
vidioholic	a person who enjoys videos very much

Evidently, being slightly changed in spelling, "alcoholic" functions as an affix to derivate new words in present-day English.

Tremendous as they are, lexical changes have never departed from the traditional ways of forming new words. This is the reason why we sometimes have to probe into modern English words by the tracing of traditional word formation.

The productivities vary from affix to affix. Studies show that affixes like *re-*, *pre-*, *on-*, *un-*, *de-*, *anti-*, *-er*, *-ness*, *-ese*, *-ism*, *-ist*, *-ics*, *-able*, *-ish*, *-less*, *-ic*, *-ise/ize*, *-ify*, etc., are the most productive ones in English. Let's take *read* for example: derivatives from it are *reread*, *pre-read*, and *reader*.

Studies on the motivations and the regulations greatly contribute to the learners' ability to analyze word formation.

4.2.3 Motivations in Abbreviation

Strictly speaking, abbreviation is a shortening of a word. But more particularly, an abbreviation is a letter or group of letters taken from a word or words, and employed to represent them for the sake of brevity.

Just as we increase the lexicon by adding or joining words together, we form new words by subtractive processes where something is taken away from the original word. The subtractive processes include clipping,

initialization, acronyms, and blends.

4.2.3.1 Clipping

Clipped words are those achieved by cutting off part of a longer word and using what remains. In everyday speech, native speakers of English often leave out parts of a word, which is also reflected in writing as well. This signifies to us, in one respect, the fact that the general course of the development of language is "simplification". Words of this kind are more often than not encountered in new English lexis. We may shorten *dormitory* to *dorm*, change *condominium* to *condo*, while using the longer term in a formal situation, and the shorter one in an informal situation. However, the new term may entirely replace the longer original word.

Many computer commands are clipped terms: to *del* means to delete, to *sho cat* means to display all the files catalogued in a particular computer account. More examples of clipped words are as follows:

auth	author
autm	autumn
auto	automobile
dorm	dormitory
flu	influenza
exam	examination
lab	laboratory
kilo	kilogram
photo	photograph
phone	telephone

Generally speaking, abbreviated words are most frequently used in an informal way, especially in everyday English. Clipped words possess some grammatical functions, suggesting that they change their forms when necessary.

4.2.3.2 Initial

Initial refers to the first letter of a word (especially a person's name) that are pronounced as separate letters. Words of this kind can be exemplified as follows:

ATM	automatic teller machine
ATV	all-terrain vehicle
VTR	video tape recorder
PIN	personal identification number
MBA	master of business administration
ASAP	as soon as possible
DNA	deoxyribonucleic acid
IOC	International Olympic Committee
WTO	World Trade Organization
VIP	very important person

4.2.3.3 Acronym

Acronym refers to the initial letters of a group of words. They are often composed of capital letters to become everyday terms. They are usually pronounced as a word instead of as separate letters. This process is widely used in shortening extremely long words or word groups in science, technology and other special fields. Words of this kind can be exemplified as follows:

SALT	Strategic Arms Limitation Talks
DINK	Double Income, No Kids
DENK	Dual Employed, No kids
NATO	North Atlantic Treaty Organization
Yuppie	Young Urban Professionals

Recently, abbreviations have become more and more popular, at

least among teenagers and young adults, partly because of mobile phones, or cell phones, which can also send text messages, but which have very limited space on their screens. So brief message abbreviations are becoming more and more common, such as IMHO (in my humble opinion) and CUL (see you later)—though caution is needed.

4.2.3.4 Blending

A blend is anything produced by mixing two or more substances together (Chambers, 1998: 99). Blending is one of the word formations in present-day English and its formation is quite unique.

Most blends are a combination of two words, with the end of the first one and the beginning of the next left out, e.g., *Chinglish*—Chinese English. Some are also formed by taking the initial part of one word and the final part of another, e.g., *carjacking*—car+hijacking.

More examples are:

brunch	breakfast+lunch
dawk	dove+hawk
gox	gas+oxygen
heliport	helicopter+airport
lox	liquid+oxygen
motel	motor+hotel
motigue	mobile+boutique
sarcastrophe	sarcasm+catastrophe
televangelist	television+evangelist
viropause	virility+menopause
smog	smoke+fog
videophone	video+telephone
fruice	fruit+juice
teleceiver	television+receiver

slanguage slang+language

Blending words are highly motivated simply because they are related with their original forms. The more easily the relation is found, the higher the motivations are.

The purpose of abbreviation is to make the form of words shorter, so as to make the expressions more direct or convenient. They are "short-cuts in language" (Seidl, J. 1978, from 汪榕培,2005:16). For this reason they are becoming more and more popular (ibid, 17).

4.2.4 Motivations in Back-formation

Back-formation (also known as reverse derivation) is the opposite process of suffixation (the formation of new words through adding suffixes to stems), which is achieved by removing the supposed suffixes. For example, we can delete *-or* from *editor* and get a new word *edit* as a verb; similarly, we have the word *automate* from *automation*.

Most English words achieved by back-formation are verbs. For example, the word *administrate* is achieved by removing the suffix *-tion* from *administration*, with a few letters slightly changed. The word *donate* is created by removing the suffix *-tion* from *donation*; the word *tack* from *tacky*; *burgle* from *burglar*; *enthuse* from *enthusiasm*; *self-destruct* from *self-destruction*, etc. There are only a few that can be used as nouns, e.g., *gloom* (n.) from *gloomy* (adj.); *greed* (n.) from *greedy* (adj.). Stylistically, these words are largely informal and among these some still have not gained public acceptance, which calls for more caution when applied in language.

4.2.5 Motivations in Borrowing

Throughout the history of language, English has been adding to its

lexicon by acquiring new words from other languages. Study shows 80% of English words are borrowed. Accordingly, when we intend to study the classes of new words, one of the immediate considerations should be around loan words.

Historically, English tended to resort to Latin and Greek. But in modern English, in the sense in which we are studying, sources of derivatives vary from culture to culture, from nation to nation, and from language to language. Until recently, English has borrowed words from almost every language of the world, such as, *hamburger* and *Ossi* derived from Germany, *kungfu*, *feng shui* and *chopsocky* from Chinese, *basuco* and *taqueria* from Spanish, *tiramisu* and *bimbo* from Italian, *fatwa* and *Hamas* from Arabian, *karaoke* and *kaizen* from Japanese, etc.

Borrowing can be carried out in different ways, i.e., direct borrowing with very little or no change to the particular word (loan word). This borrowing can be carried out by translating the loan word into the one already available in the language, known as a loan translation; or by combining a loan word and an already existing word called a loan blend, while the extension or a change in the meaning of existing words in the language is a loan shift.

Loan translation, loan blend, and loan shift are the products of assimilated loan words. Sometimes they should follow the rules of the language they come into with the characteristics of the language they come from. In a word, they are the mixture of two languages. After being adopted in a different language system, new loan words generally undergo one or more of the following transformations: phonetic, semantic, and structural.

A well-known example would be the word *sputnik*, a popular

Russian word, which has been used to produce many new English words like *computernik*, *no-goodnik*, *beatnik*, *folknik*, *peacenik*, etc.; partly borrowed from Russian. Words like *humburger*, *beefburger*, *steakburger*, *turkeyburger*, *cheeseburger*, *fishberger*, *nutburger*, *turkeyburger*, *clam-burger*, *muttonburger*, *shrimpburger*, *nothingburger* are partly borrowed from Germany.

Why do speakers borrow words from other languages? The main reason for linguistic borrowing is to fill a void in the borrowing language to describe new concepts and elements. People need to create words for new and unfamiliar concepts—new events, new places, new technology, new inventions and new and unfamiliar foods, etc. The fact that we lack the words with these new concepts in vocabulary encourages us to borrow words. Another reason might be that since loan words are quite direct and easily acceptable among young people, who are usually the representatives of the new, loan words become one part of new English words.

Prestige could also be considered a reason for the borrowing of words. Continuing with the food theme, France was at one time considered the center of world gastronomy, and hence English has words like *gourmet*, *cuisine*, *restaurant*, *menu* and *soup*, which have been borrowed from the French language.

4.2.6 Motivations in Coinage

Every language has its native words that have not been borrowed from other languages, but that have developed with the language over time. What happens when neither borrowed words nor native words are available? One of the solutions is to coin a new or unique word.

Coinages are newly invented words or expressions. A word or

phrase can be coined outright to meet certain needs in a certain situation, or at a certain time.

4.2.6.1 Coined Antonyms

A new word can also be coined by replacing the existed morpheme in a word with a new morpheme antonymous. These words formed by contrast are called coined antonyms. For example:

nightmare	daymare
hot line	cold line
baby boom	baby bust
upstream	downstream
upmarket (market where products with high quality are sold)	downmarket
boycott	girlcott
call girl	call boy
DINK (double income and no kids)	SINK (single income and no kids)

Rhetorically, they belong to the words formed by analogy, however, as one part of the internal motivations in words, they are called coined antonyms.

4.2.6.2 Coined Synonyms

Rhetorically, many new words of this kind can be coined in a form of initials. For example:

WWW, *HTTP*, *URL*, *PPS* (pocket phone service), *CD* (compact disc), *VCD* (video-compact disc), *DVD* (digital video disc, digital versatile disc), *VTR* (video tape recorder), *VCR* (video cassette recorder). Other examples would include the following:

frostbelt	snowbelt
King's English	Queen's English

yuppie	yippie
CD	VCD

4.2.6.3　Words Formed by Analogy

Sometimes, a new word can be coined by replacing the morpheme in a word with a new one, and the meaning of this morpheme is analogous to the one in the existing word. Thus motivation is produced in the process of analogy.

For example: the new expression *brain drain* can not only be coined by contrasting i.e., *brain gain*, but also be analogized into the followings:

brain gain	brain drain
brain drain	brawn drain
white-collar worker	blue-collar worker (physical laborer) pink-collar worker (those whose occupations involve teachers, salesgirls, nurses and secretaries) steel-collar worker (robot)
bird's eye view	fish-eye view (180° view) worm's eye view (upward view)
greenbelt	snowbelt (frostbelt) frostbelt (northern part of the US) sunbelt (southern part of the US)
green revolution	blue revolution (ugly and dirty deals by the decadent school's) gray revolution
Silicon Plain (Texas, US)	Silicon Valley Silicon Island (Kyushu, Japan) Silicon Desert (around Arizona, US)

	baby boom
	baby sitter
baby bust	baby-batterer (person who batter a baby)
	baby-minder (person paid to look after a baby for long periods)
	VCD
CD	DVD
	VTR
	VCR

From the perspective of internal motivations, they are called coined synonyms.

4.2.7 Motivations in Some Letter Groups

When studying the phonetics and word formation, we find that there does exist some relationship between the sound of some letter groups and its semantic meaning. For example, The letter group *fl-* as in the word *flicker* seems to be related to light or flare. More examples as in *flame*, *flare*, *flash* can provide supporting evidence. The letter group *fl-*also implies the movement or flaring of a light or flare, as in *flee*, *fleet*, *float*, *flounce*, *flow*, *fluctuate*, *flutter*, *fluent*, *fluid*, *flurry*, *flux* and *fly*. Some linguists call this phenomenon the sound symbolism (汪榕培, 1999: 136). In Wang's book *Gems of English Vocabulary*, many examples are cited to prove that the letter group *sl-* implies the movement of sliding, as in *slant*, *sled*, *sleek*, *slick*, *slide*, *slime*, *slip*, *slither*, *slope*, *slop*, *slosh*, *slough*, *slur*, *slush*, *sly* and so on.

What is mentioned above is also called minor phonological motivations in words, that is, an indirect relationship between the sound and its semantic meaning. Since this part also involves the morphemes, each of which represents a different morphologic type, it is also classified into the combined motivations of phonology and morphology.

Bloomfield (1935: 245) brought forward 17 morphologic types in his *Language*, where he suggests more details including the following:

(1)fl-, "moving light": flash, flare, flame, flicker

(2) gl-, "unmoving light": glow, glare, gloat, gloom, gleam, gloaming, glimmer, glint

(3)sn-, "breath-noise": sniff, snuff, snore, snort, snot

(4)sn-, "creeping": snake, snail, sneak, snoop

(5)j-, "up-and-down movement": jump, jounce, jig, jog, juggle, jangle, jingle

(6)-ash, "violent movement": bash, clash, crash, dash, flash, gash, mash, gnash, slash, splash

(7)-are, "big light or noise": blare, flare, glare, stare

(8)-ounce, "quick movement": bounce, jounce, pounce, trounce

(9)-ump, "clumsy": bump, clump, chump, dump, frump, hump, lump, rump, stump, slump, thump.

...

Since there are various rules to follow in word formation, motivations in this sense are very high.

4.3 Summary

Morphologically speaking, as a phonological system, English has been studied mainly from the perspective of word formation, particularly by Western linguists. In this case, morphological motivations in new English lexis possess some characteristics which are more imitative, (such as *Bushnomics*, *Clintonomics*, *Reagonomics*, *Rogernomics*,

Thatchernomics, etc.). Also included is the abbreviated form, such as AL (artificial intelligence), PC (personal computer), ER (emergency room), VCD (video compact disc), BE (best friend) and more casual (to better, to house, to weekend). Some Chinese linguists creatively began to take a keen insight into English lexis from a pictographic point of view, since the Chinese lexis is a pictographic system. Combined with Chinese characteristics, studies of the English language are more likely to have more creative academic findings. Though English language is a phonological system, it possesses, at least partly, some pictographic motivations. The reason why Chinese linguists have achieved some academic findings in the study of pictographic motivations of English lexis is that languages possess similarities, and that "our shared experience of the world is also stored in our everyday language and can thus be gleaned from the way we express our ideas" (Ungerer, 38). The fresh viewpoint of some Chinese linguists, though controversial, is worth encouraging instead of frustrating, for any encouragements will likely lead to more findings.

The study on morphological motivations of new English lexis deals only with linguistic signs themselves, that is, the internal study of linguistic signs. The study on semantic motivations of linguistic signs in the following chapter covers both internal and external study of linguistic signs. It tackles the meanings or senses of words as well as the word formation.

Chapter Five Semantic Motivations of New English Lexis

Semantic motivations refer to the motivations based on semantic factors (Feng Shi-mei, 2003). It is a kind of mental association based on the conceptual meaning of a word, which is considered the figurative sense of the word. This indicates that the motivations are achieved by resorting to the basic semantic meanings, the background knowledge of the words, and by inducing the further meaning (汪榕培, 2002: 1). Many of them have undergone extraordinary semantic changes. Or they can, to a large extent, be semantically motivated.

Semantic motivations can be roughly classified into two major categories: the internal (linguistic) one and the external one (see Figure 5-1). The former refers to the linguistic changes taking place because of linguistic phenomena, while the latter refers to the semantic changes occurring because of non-linguistic phenomena. Since internal changes have been investigated in the chapter of morphological motivations, we need only to explore the external changes in semantics.

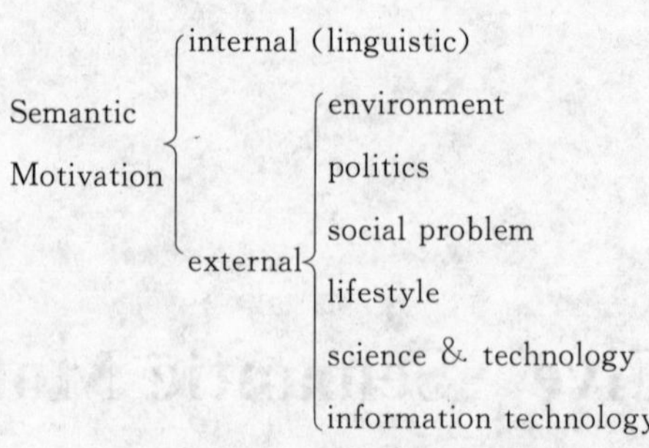

Figure 5-1 Semantic motivation

5.1 Political Motivation

5.1.1 Statesman Motivation

Politics provides one of the important sources of new words, as its influence on the English vocabulary is as great as that of other factors, which deserves particular concern.

As centered roles in the American politics, American presidents contribute a lot to the emergence of new American English words. As mentioned above, when *Reaganism* (the policies and principles advocated by Ronald Reagan in 1966) appeared, the new word *Reaganite* (a member of Reagan team) was coined, followed by *Reaganomics* (the economic policies of President Ronald Reagan, especially the conservative view that fiscal responsibility rests primarily with private industry and the states rather than the national government). Another political word, *Reaganaut*, meaning an ardent supporter of the policies of Ronald Reagan, is a much used political word. Others such as *Reaganite*, *Reaganomical*, *Reaganomically*, *Reagan democrat*, *Reaganize*, and *Reaganesque*, are related to the policies of Ronald Reagan. *Reaganology*, which is a study of the policies of President

Ronald Reagan, especially his conservative political and economic policies including cutting back the size of the national government and strengthening the military forces (陆国强, 2000: 1022-1023), etc.

Words related to Bill Clinton can be largely exemplified, when he beat his opponent and became the US president, particularly since 1997. The word *Clintonite*, denoting "of Bill Clinton, which implies a new philosophy that would break with the conservatism of the Reagan years" (Ayto, 2002). The word *Clintonism* refers to the policies that Clinton carried out. The success of *Clintonism* was chiefly due to the period in which Clinton governed and to his remarkable political skills, but not to the electoral strategy he bequeathed to his party. The economical policy he carried out was *Clintonomics*. Those who supported him were *Clintonites*, *Clintonians*, or *Clintonoids*. Even his sexscandal was called the *Clinton sexscandal*.

In contrast, *Bushonomics* or *Perotnomics* doesn't quite make it.

When John Major became the Prime Minister of Great Britain, there appeared *Majorism* (the policy of Major) and his supporters *Majorites*, followed by *Blairism*, *Blairist*, *Blairite* and so on.

5.1.2 Scandal Motivation

English vocabulary extends quickly not only by the influential statesmen, but also by places where some political or social events took place. As well as stories of virtue, the scandals of influential people were recorded and started to emerge into the English vocabulary.

Originally, "Watergate", referred to the Watergate Hotel in Washington, D.C., and was later a political scandal involving abuse of power, bribery and obstruction of justice. Reasons can be traced to the US Presidential Election in 1972. Before the Election, in order to stand a

dominating position in election to the Democratic Party, National Committee officials attempted to install bugging devices in the telephones of Democrats. With the scandal exposed to light, Nixon became the first president in American history to resign from office. From then on, *Watergate Affair* became a general term used to describe a complex web of political scandals.

As a political scandal, *Watergate Affair* caused a great stir in the world for a long period of time. Greatly affected in language, the synonyms with the suffix *-gate* kept dramatically increasing in number. For example, the incident that an oil company in England sold oil to racialists in North Africa was called *Oilgate*. Even in recent times, the story of how South Africa's ruling party "offered solidarity" to Iraq leader Saddam Hussein in exchange for crude oil and how State resources were used to help the party in this project became known as *Oilgate*. The case that one of the chemical companies located in Michigan, USA, once mixed poisons with feed additives, which poisoned many cattle was called *Cattlegate*. The affair that the USA former president Jimmy Carter's brother, Billy Carter, once accepted payment for goods to commit illegal affairs was called *Billygate*. More than twenty years ago, the incident that top operatives in Ronald Reagan's presidential campaign helped coach Reagan for a crucial debate with Carter by making the most of the illegally obtained papers, and won a thoroughbred performance was labeled *debategate*. The Iran-Contra Affair was also known as *Irangate*, in which President Ronald Reagan's administration sold arms to Iran, an avowed enemy. Years ago, when the sexual scandal about US former President Clinton and Lewinsky was revealed, that was known as *zippergate*. From the new dictionary of English neologisms, we could find more words with *-gate* as in *Briefing-gate*, *cookiegate*,

Contragate, *copygate*, *gibberishgate*, *Godsgate*, *Gospelgate*, *Guinnessgate*, *harborgate*, *Heavengate*, *Inkathagage*, *Keelgate*, *Koreagate*, *Pageantgate*, *Pearlgate*, *pseudo-gate*, *Reagangate*, *salvationgate*, *Sewergate*, *Sharongate*, *Stargate*, *sugargate*, *targate*, *Totegate*, *Walk-on-gate*, etc.

In fact, after *Watergate Affair*, new words with the suffix *-gate*, bearing the implication of "scandals", appeared one after another not only in the English vocabulary, but also in other languages. We can safely conclude *-gate* has already been an actual suffix in word building.

5.1.3 Political Event Motivation

Like political scandals, political events have also provided people with a wide horizon to form new words and innovative expressions. As an important part of the English vocabulary, the development of the English vocabulary owes a great debt to them.

After World War II, there appeared a great variety of political and counter-culture movements, which helped to create many new words like *hippie*, *yippie*, *hippydom*, *beatnik*, *dropout*, etc. *The Sex Lib movement* encouraged the appearance of *mingles*, *pansexual*, *striptease*, *streaking*, *ambidextrous*, *youthquake*, *commune*, etc.

A noteworthy phenomenon is the combining form of the adverb *in* introduced in the 1960s by the African American civil rights movement. The word *sit-in* originally appeared in 1937. It basically refers to "a strike, demonstration, etc., in which people occupy a work place, public building, etc., especially in protest against alleged activities there". (Ayto, 2002: 291) In the 1960s, the combining of the adverb "in" was introduced by the African American civil rights movement. It was triggered by an anti-White event, which occurred in 1960, when four black students of the Greenshore Agriculture and Technical College in North Carolina went to a Woolworth's store for a cup of coffee. The waiter refused to serve them simply because they were black. When the students insisted on being served, they were taken away; thus a new series of words denoting a protest came into being, as follows:

lie-in: an act of lying down (as in a public place) in organized protest or as a means of forcing compliance with demands.

kneel-in: the act of entering a white-only church to do service.

ride-in: the act of getting on a bus which is for the white only.

swim-in: the act of swimming in a swimming pool which is for the white only.

sleep-in: the act of occupying of a public place by a group of people to sleep there as a form of protest.

Later, words or expressions with *-in* suffix developed. A number of "v. + *-in*" words came into the American vocabulary and flowed from the lips of African Americans frequently. The original meaning extended soon to the staging of any kind of public demonstration. For example:

smoke-in: a demonstration for the legalization of smoking marijuana.

Still later, the earlier meaning weakened and, as a result, it covered almost any kind of gathering. This meaning is exemplified by the words *be-in*. Other such words are contained in the following:

teach-in: a meeting held by university teachers for the purpose of criticizing a social issue.

work-in: a form of demonstration in which a group of people report to work but disregard the rules.

sing-in: a musical event in which the audience serves as a chorus.

eat-in: a dinner party.

phone-in: a radio or television program centered around people who call the studio by telephone to ask questions or air opinions.

The Feminist Movement motivates the appearance of new words like *feminism*, *chauvinism*, *Women's Lib*, *Sexism*, *Ms.*, etc. Many words with gender bias like *chairman*, *fireman*, and *airhostess* were replaced with *chairperson*, *fire fighter* and *flight attendant*.

During the 1960s, the counter-war movement contributed to the emergence of some new words like *peacenik*, *Vietnik*, *daftnik*, etc.

On September 11th, 2001, the world witnessed an unprecedented attack against the United States, in which the Twin Towers of the World Trade Center in New York collapsed over one hour after two planes crashed into them. Since President Bush declared a war on terror, phrases such as *the war on terrorism*, and *the war on terror*, have been added to English expressions. When the US Senate condemned the abuse to Iraqi prisoners and demanded an apology to the victims by American soldiers, *prisoner abuse scandal*, and *Iraqi prisoner abuse* became new expressions.

The new word *ECU* is an abbreviation for *European Currency Unit*. It is a monetary unit created in 1979 by nine European nations to promote currency stability within the European Union.

The *European Monetary System* (EMS) is an exchange-rate system adopted by European Union members in an effort to move toward a unified European currency.

The new expression *nuclear winter* appeared in 1983. It refers to "a period of extreme cold and devastation that has been conjectured to follow a nuclear war, caused by an atmospheric layer of smoke and dust particles shutting out the Sun's rays". (ibid, 679)

The new expression *Third World* appeared in 1963. It refers to "the countries of the world, especially those of Africa and Asia, which during

the *Cold War* were aligned with neither the Communist nor the non-Communist bloc, hence the underdeveloped or poorer countries of the world, usually those of Africa, Asia, and Latin America" (ibid, 548).

5. 2 Social Problem Motivation

As societies change and develop, many social problems arise. For example, more and more females frequently suffer both physical and verbal harassment, a case that is quite common, but very annoying, like frequently receiving some ugly mobile phone short messages and junk e-mails. The word, *harassment* or *sexual harassment*, has emerged into not only English, but also other language vocabularies. Even in China, the draft amendment of *Law on the Protection of Rights and Interests of Women* will introduce definitions of *sexual harassment* and ultimately lead to the arrest and punishment of offenders.

Meanwhile, with the development of society, and the introduction of new science and technology, man's life is getting better and better. This directly leads to another social problem—*the age issue*.

Granny Dumping, which is defined as the abandonment of elderly relatives by their caretakers, is another social problem especially in Western countries. This word was coined in the US in the early 1990s when case that elderly people were deserted by their caretakers and left in hospitals or nursing homes happened.

While *monogyny* is regarded as a dominant family style in modern society, *common-law marriage*, *single-parent household*, *un-wed mother*, *covenant marriage*, *trial marriage*, *consensual no monogamy*, *communard*, etc., continue to exist.

We are so familiar with the odd phenomenon—*homosexuality*,

however, there is an opposite one, "*Persons of Opposite Sex Sharing Living Quarters*", a term coined in the late 1970s by the United States Census Bureau as part of an effort to more accurately measure the prevalence of cohabitation in American households. Its abbreviation (or acronym) *POSSLQ* is the typical new English word. After the 1980 census, against all odds, the term (pronounced "poss-el-cue") gained popularity in more cultures for a time. By the 1990s, the term had fallen out of general usage, and returned to being a specialized term for experts.

The world is full of happiness and sadness. In order to escape from the devastating real world, in order to be "immediately happy and excited", some people, especially young adults and even some teenagers resort to using drugs. Under such circumstances, the new term *drug use* has come into being.

In the early 1990s, when the United States experienced a decade of extraordinary economic prosperity, economic growth had been steady and vigorous. Although the overall economic growth benefited the whole country, indications showed that it led directly to another dramatic rise in *income inequality*. Meanwhile, the largest income gains have come to those in the top income and wealth brackets.

5.3 Environmental Motivation

Environmental changes not only affect the physical surroundings, but also greatly influence languages. Up to now, *Environmental Protection* still remains the heated topic in modern world. The first *Conference on Environment and Development of the World* was held in Stockholm in 1972. In 1992, as a milestone in the sustainable

development of the world, the second United Nations Conference on Environment and Development was held in Rio de Janeiro, Brazil. The conference adopted several important documents, including Rio Declaration on Environment and Development and Agenda 21 and Earth Charter. This conference was called *Earth Summit*. In the conference, *carbon tax* was also under discussion.

Environment protectionists proclaim the limitation on the use of natural resources. They demand that wise use of natural resources reduce the *ecological footprint*. They suggest that we should have *an energy audit* on the household energy consumption and use *blue boxes* for *garbage reusing*. They also advocate that we install *speed humps*, *speed bumps* or *road humps* which would force drivers to slow down as a guide to *calming traffic*, that we use *alternative fuel*, *superunleaded* or *bio-diesel* instead of gasoline, to diminish *air pollution*, *heat/thermal pollution*, *internal pollution*, *visual pollution*. Those who are in favor of *green peace* are often called *tree huggers*, while others are known as *fundies*. The new slang word *fundies*, makes reference to people who would live in a tree house or *twigloo*, rather than in their apartments for the sake of sustainable natural resources.

5.4 New Lifestyle Motivation

Different lifestyles have created individuals with different characteristics and values. Some become *Mr. Clean* (one who is morally or sexually pure, honorable or free from guilt), while some become *Mr. Right* (the most suitable person or object). Others become *Mr. Fix* (one who is good at fixing), or *Mr. Sick* (one who makes people sick). Among other new labels are *Mr. Crouch* (one who complains a lot), or

Mr. Hasbeen (one whose thoughts are behind times). What makes them unique from others are their different lifestyles.

5.4.1 Health Motivation

New healthy lifestyles benefit those who enjoy it; meanwhile, new unhealthy lifestyles often bring troubles or even disasters to those who indulge or over indulge themselves. In the 20th century, some of those who indulged themselves in homosexual activities have suffered the most horrible illness, *AIDS*.

The new expression *AIDS virus* was coined in 1983. Those volunteering to help persons with AIDS are *buddies*. Many medical researchers are trying to find an *AIDS vaccine*, which would be made available in the forms of *chemotherapy* and *chemoprevention*.

Air conditioners enable us to live in artificial surroundings, however, we may easily suffer from the *SBS* (*sick building syndrome*). For some unknown reason, some people may get *RSI* (*repetitive strain injury*), *necrotizing fasciitis* or *flesh-eating disease*. There are also more new illnesses like *ADD* (*attention deficit disorder*), *SAD* (*seasonal affective disorder*), *PTSD* (*post-traumatic stress disorder*), *recovered memory syndrome*, *false memory syndrome*, which we had never heard of until recently.

The new expression *birth control pill* was created in 1966.

The new word *DNA*, an abbreviation of Deoxyribonucleic acid, denotes "an illness in which opportunistic infections or malignant tumours develops as a result of a severe loss of cellular immunity..." (ibid, 640). The new expression *genetic fingerprinting* created in 1984 is called *DNA fingerprinting* (1969), meaning a genetic fingerprint obtained by examination of DNA (ibid, 246).

The new expression *Gulf War Syndrome* appeared in 1992. It refers to "a syndrome of uncertain cause including fatigue, joint pain, memory loss, skin rash, and headache that has been reported in veterans of the war fought in the Persian Gulf in 1991".

The new expression *mad cow disease* (*BSE or bovine spongiform encephalopathy*) was created in 1988. When the disease first appeared in Europe, it severely affected the beef industry around the world.

The new word *SARS*, an abbreviation of severe acute respiratory syndrome, appeared in 2003. It is also known as atypical pneumonia, an expression used in China since 2003.

Presently, the *bird flu* is spreading throughout the world.

5.4.2 Leisure and Entertainment Motivation

With more and more working class getting busier and busier, an ever-increasing number of *mobile phones* are now available instead of telephones. These are used whether at work or at home, and were considered a novelty item one or two decades ago.

Life is usually busy and full of pressure. When at work, some have to wear *power dressing* instead of *street style* clothing. They can hardly take *a power nap* and can seldom enjoy their *quality time*. On weekends, they usually hire a *home-sitter* or *house-sitter* to do housework or a *baby-sitter* to look after babies so that they can enjoy some form of tourism. For children at home, the *gogglebox*, *idiot box*, or *idiot's lantern* is absolutely safe. They may even warm food in a *microwave oven* with an *autotimer* attached to it. Mothers can go to the *warehouse club* to shop for some *ambient food* in an *ambient warehouse* and they can enjoy *home shopping*, *electronic shopping* or on-line shopping even at home. Then they can watch *Videos* in the *home cinema* or *home theatre*. They can make a *videophone* or *picturephone call*, while they enjoy some *soap operas* during *prime time*. If they miss it, they can enjoy the *instant replay* on the *VTR*, or *VCR*.

As we all know, technology has contributed a lot to our everyday life and made our leisure time more enjoyable. For instance, watching TV has become the dominant pastime for many people, however, people are not satisfied with what they have. They are longing for more exciting entertainment venues, such as *Bungee Jumping*, *extreme skiing*, and *cable skiing*. They may participate in *jet-skiing*, *heli-skiing*, *hydro speeding*, or *snowboarding* from which they obtain the maximum satisfaction or thrill.

Some sports toys like *skydive*, *land/sand yacht*, *hang glider*, etc., are the more advanced ones, while other new activities like *cycle-cross*, *roller hockey*, *demolition derby*, *slimnastics*, *isometrics*, etc., have also gained more and more popularity.

5.5 New Product Motivation

Social economy is considered the mother of human civilization. Without commercial activities, the social economy would not have been under development, let alone social civilizations! In commercial activities, products as well as its advertisements play an important role. In almost every part of the world, particularly in some Western countries, commercial advertisements seem to be everywhere. Accordingly, words that appear in ads leave a deep impression in the mind; therefore, new words come out as a result of ad words, which gradually gain wide acceptance and popularity. For example, *Coca-Cola* is a brand of a carbonated soft drink of the Kola Company in US, which

became a worldwide product during the 20th century. However, "Coca" once witnessed a long-time lawsuit for its brand privilege. Eventually, the Coca Cola Company succeeded in winning the lawsuit. In 1945, Coca Cola Company got the registered trademark: Coca.

Since Cola was not registered then, Caleb D. Bradham successfully developed and later registered a beverage named *Pepsi-Cola*. From then on, beverages with the suffix *-cola* sprang up like *Royal Crown Cola* (*RC*), *Future Cola*, etc. The new *colacolaizational* words with new senses widely spread to the other parts of the world, e.g., the *Chinese Tian Fu Cola*, *Shao Lin Cola*, a radio program named *Breakfast Cola*, *Coca-colonize*, *Coca-colonization*, etc. Even though Coca is defined as "a carbonated soft drink containing an extract made from Kola nuts" (Gerard, 1998: 256), its implication is far beyond.

Another case in point is *hamburger*, which was originally borrowed from the German language. During the mid 19th century, with the immigration of Germans, meals named after hamburger were immigrated into the United States. Soon, it gained nationwide acceptance for its reasonable price, pleasant taste and convenient cooking. Under the influence of *hamburgers*, a large variety of burgers showed up in food stores of the US in late 20th Century, like *beefburger*, *steakburger*, *turkeyburger*, *cheeseburger*, *fishberger*, *nutburger*, *clam-burger*, *muttonburger*, *shrimpburger*, and even *nothingburger* (a cake with no fillings). The meaning of *nothingburger* gradually went so far that it partly implies "something boring or invaluable". That's the influence food brought to languages.

When classifying the naming motivations in brands, Wang Feng-xin (王逢鑫, 2003: 393) concluded six: the names of the inventors, the birthplaces of the goods, the functions of the products, the echoes of the native pronunciation, the images of the brand and the concepts they represent. Having taken advantage of them by translating into other languages, many firms have succeeded in occupying the global markets.

5.6 Scientific and Technological Motivation

People cannot avoid encountering new things or conveying new concepts, even for a day. New words and expressions enter the language with new ideas or new concepts in the ever-developing society. Modern science and technology bring about the addition of new words in unlimited numbers. They are the most important source of new words. In other words, science and technology are the main source of this new vocabulary. Modern science and technology contain many new branches apart from some existing fields, with the appearance of new branches in modern science and technology giving rise to a great number of new words.

For example, the new word *biomineralization* was coined in 1973. It refers to "the formation or accumulation of minerals by organisms especially into biological tissues or structures (as bones, teeth and shells)".

The new word *biomimetics* appeared in 1974. It means "the study of the formation, structure, or function of biologically produced substances and materials and biological mechanisms and processes especially for the purpose of synthesizing similar products by artificial mechanisms which mimic natural ones".

The new expression *media study* was coined in the 1980s. It refers to "the collection, classification, storage, retrieval, and dissemination of recorded knowledge treated both as a pure and as an applied science".

With human beings successfully landing on the moon in 1969, there emerged a series of new words like *moonik*, *moonwalk*, *moonman*, *moonfall*, *moonscape*, *moonrock*, *mooncraft*, *moonport*, *moonset*, *moonship*, *moon shoot*, *lunar rover*, etc.

To *dock*, which originally meant, "to sail into a place where ships are loaded or unloaded" has acquired a new meaning "the linkup of spacecraft in space". Since the launching of a spaceship represents the scientific development of mankind, understandingly, we now come across so many new words in connection with it, such as *space sickness*, *space suit*, *space travel*, *space walk*, *space age*, *space cadet*, *space colony*, *space industry*, *spacelift*, *space race*, *space science*, *deep space*, *neutron star*, and *black hole*. More words or expressions are as follows: *astronaut*, *spacecraft*, *spaceflight*, *spaceport*, *space station*, *spaceman*, *space medicine*, *space opera*, etc.

The new word *spacewalk* is a verb occurring in 1965 (meaning "to move about outside a spacecraft in space"). The new word *space walker* created in 1965 refers to "an astronaut who moves about outside a spacecraft in space". The new expression *space shuttle* appeared in 1969, referring to "a reusable spacecraft to transport people and cargo between earth and space".

On Oct. 4, 1957, when the Soviet Union succeeded in launching *Sputnik I*, history changed. As a technical achievement, Sputnik caught the world's attention. Linguistically speaking, the Sputnik launch also led directly to the appearance of more words with *-nik* suffix as follows:

goodwillnik:	a person who has kind feelings towards other people
no-goodnik:	an unreliable or despicable person
arcadenik:	a habitué of video-game arcades
beatnik:	hippie in the 50s of the 20th century

computernik: a computer enthusiast or expert
folknik: a folk song singer
peacenik: an active opponent of war
Vietnik: a person who opposed US

In recent forty years or so, owing to the gigantic development in genetics, fresh new words and expressions like *genetic code*, *DNA* (Deoxyribonucleic Acid), *transfer RNA* (Ribonucleic Acid), *messenger RNA*, and *transcription* are becoming more and more popular day by day. Only a few years ago, it might come as something terribly frightening that some scientists have succeeded in "*cloning*" people.

New words in English, expressively, belong to lexical words or content words, which mainly involve nouns, adjectives, verbs, and adverbs, which in the end possess variability. Since new words of this kind endlessly keep increasing in number and in principle, they belong to open-class words. With the development of society and with the emergence of new ideas, and new inventions, it is just like a new stream of fresh blood to be injected into English vocabulary. The English language will become more active, more energetic and more vigorous, with the addition of these new words.

5.7 New Information Motivation

We are living in the so-called Information Age, an age in which new information spreads very rapidly and is shared by more people from different fields of endeavor. Every day, people, including adults and children, use computers to learn and gain knowledge of happenings in the world. As a universal language, English has helped the spread and transfer of information, therefore, a great number of new words

concerning computers appear constantly in modern English. Many new words, as well as new meanings, have developed out of the Information Age, such as the following:

The word *agent* is an existing word, but now it has a new meaning: a computer application designed to automate certain tasks (as gathering information online). The new word *computernik* composed of "computer +*-nik*", a suffix denoting a person, appeared in 1968, meaning "a computer enthusiast or expert". The new word *computerphobe* coined in 1976 refers to "a person who experiences anxiety about computers and especially about their use". Here *-phobe* is a combining form, meaning "a person who has a certain fear, hatred or terror".

The new word *CNN* is an abbreviation for Cable News Network used in the United States.

The new word *e-mail* or *E-mail* created in 1982 is a shortened form of electronic mail, which was coined in 1975.

The new expression *Generation D* comes from an abbreviation of digital generation that denotes "the generation of people with great interest or expertise in computers and other digital devices, e.g., technology marketers focus *Generation D*".

The new expression *Generation* X was coined in 1991, denoting "a generation of young people perceived to be disaffected, directionless, and having no part to play in society" or "a 'lost generation'" (Ayto. J. 2002: 721).

The new word *cyber* used as an adjective, means "relating to computers or computer network". The word *cybernetics* was coined in 1948, defined as "a field of study that compares the control and communication systems of the body with mechanical or electronic systems of control and communication" (Dalgish, 1977: 342). Since then, many words with the prefix *cyber-* have been invented one after another, for example, *cybernaut*, *cybersurfer*, *cyber mania*, *cyber source*, *cyber bar*, *cyber culture*, *cyberpunk*, *cyberpet*, *cyberspace*, etc. *Cybercafe* was coined in 1994, referring to "a café or coffee shop providing computers for access to the Internet". *Cybercitizen* comes from *netizen*, a blend of "net" and "citizen", which appeared in 1994.

The new word *hyperinflation* was coined in 1930, followed by *hyperdrive* in 1955, *hypermedia* in 1965, *hyperlink* in 1988. It denotes an electronic link providing access from one distinctively marked place in a *hypertext* or *hypermedia* document to another in the same or a different document.

The new word *multimedia* appeared in 1967. It means "of or being a form of artistic, educational, or commercial communication in which more than one medium is used" (Ayto, 2002: 521).

The word *mouse* is an existing word, but with a new sense added to it, meaning "a small mobile manual device that controls movement of the cursor and selection of functions on a computer display".

The new expression *search engine* appeared in 1984. It is "a system for searching the information available on the Web".

The new word *download* serves as a verb appeared in 1980. It means "to transfer (esp. software) from the storage of a larger computer system to that of a smaller one" (Ayto, 2002: 656). The new word *upload* used as a verb appeared in 1983. It means "to transfer data or files from a computer to the memory of another device".

The new word *webcam*, made up of "web + camera" appeared in 1995, is a camera used in transmitting live images over the World Wide Web. The new word *webcast*, a blend of "World Wide Web + broadcast" coined in 1995, means "a transmission of sound and images via the World

Wide web". The new word *webmaster* appearing in 1994, refers to "a person responsible for the creation or maintenance of a Web site especially for a company or organization".

The new expression *global village*, coined in 1960, is "a term popularized by Marshall MacLhan (1911—1980) for the world in the age of high technology and international communications, through which events throughout the world may be experienced simultaneously by everyone, so apparently 'shrinking' world societies to the level of a single village or tribe" (Ayto, 2002: 503). This word became even more fashionable after Hillary Clinton published her best selling book, *It Takes a Village*.

Thanks to the development in science and technology, the media is transforming itself on all fronts. *DBS* (satellite television) arrived, and dishes sprouted all over the world. *Infotainment* (information treated as entertainment, such as *call-in*, *chat show*, *commercial concert*, *current affairs*, etc.) is on offer, and *rolling news* (complete with sound bites) is enjoyed. Alternatively, if you have a *camcorder*, you could make a video of your own, or if you owed a *MP3 player*, a *walkman*, or a *CD player*, you might take the sound with you wherever you go. If you posses an inviting *MP4 player*, then videos would become portable. If you had a *PC camera* and a *computer* attached to the *Internet*, you might chat with people anywhere, for the mixture of them is multi functional, such as a video telephone, if those people on the other side had both a PC camera and a computer. It costs much less when compared with making a telephone call. Since the high-speed computer network, with the Internet as its core, has come into existence, the Internet has become the most important and the largest store for knowledge.

5.8 Summary

Semantic motivations in words are closely associated with history and cultures. Semantic motivations in English words, as well as in other languages, represent the commonalities and similarities of the world. In this sense, semantic motivations in any linguistic signs can be concluded to be the same or similar. Specifically speaking, most countries have different histories and more diverse cultures, with their semantically motivated backgrounds being somewhat different. Hence, newly coined words may vary from language to language, from form to form, and from motivation to motivation. Each possesses its own characteristics. As for new English lexis, it possesses some unique characteristics apart from the ones shared by general English lexis.

New words related to the computer technology and the Internet account for the largest proportion of newly coined words, most of which are American English words. This is due to the high development of information technology in the US.

In addition, when compared with other languages, the political, scientific and technological influences on language in the US are more profound than that in any other countries. This is also due to the advanced science and technology.

In conclusion, it is the advantage or superiority in science and technology that makes the nation more powerful, thus making its language more influential, regardless of history.

Chapter Six Psychological Motivations of New English Lexis

The study on motivations of English lexis might be conducted from a psychological angle. This is because the way the new lexis is formed, not only reflects man's physical activities like social, political or historical events, but also mirror the inner world of man's mind, including his mental activities and cognition. Studies on this issue not only help to investigate the psychological system of languages, but also help to introduce the computational models of the grammatical processes in both language comprehension and speech production. The study might be very helpful in bilingual teaching and learning.

By investigating motivations of new English lexis, we find the creation or appearance of a new word largely depends on man's frame of mind.

6.1 Fashion Pursuing Tendencies of Mind

People tend to pursue not only fashionable dress, but also fashionable expressions in language. To some extent, people's turn of mind regarding fashions, linguistically contributes to the appearance of an increasing English vocabulary. When *yuppie*[①] came into existence in the 1970s, more and more new words coined in this way rushed into the English vocabulary due to its fresh and fashionable formation, which greatly appeals to the people's turn of mind, like:

Buppie: black urban professionals

Yippie: youth international party

Yeepie: youthful energetic people involved in everything

Yappie: young affluent professional

Woopie: well-off old people

Sippie: senior independent pioneers

Zuppie: zestful upscale people in their prime

Zippie: zen-inspired propoia pagans

Guppie: gay urban professionals

Hippie: Home Instruction for Parents of Preschool Youngsters

When *Reaganism* was coined, some newly coined synonyms such as *Reaganomics*, *Reaganaut*, *Reagan democrat*, *Reaganize*, *Reaganesque*, *Reaganology*, etc., followed. Some of the words we create or coin does not necessarily stay forever. Some may remain, while others may die out. And some may develop their meanings by broadening and elevating, while others may go out of existence. This is a natural tendency of languages' development.

① An abbreviation for young urban professionals, referring to a young city or suburban resident with a well-paid professional job and an affluent lifestyle. (http://www.thefreedictionary.com/yuppie)

6. 2 Elegance Seeking Tendencies of Mind

Normally, people prefer to use mild, agreeable language when talking about an unpleasant or embarrassing incident (such as death, disease, unfortunate events or crime), and of taboo subjects such as sex and the excretive processes of the body. This state of mind leads to euphemisms. For example, people use "to pass away", "to breathe one's last", "to cease to think", "to fall asleep", "to go west", "to kick the bucket", "to be no more", etc., to imply "to die". They use "handicapped" instead of "crippled". They tend to avoid using dirty words, which usually refer to taboo subjects such as sex and excretion, in civilized community. For example, they use euphemisms such as "to go to the toilet/bathroom/lavatory" or "to wash one's hands" instead of "to urinate". They use "experienced people" or "senior citizens" instead of "the old". They use "strong" for "fat". They choose *cosmetologist* as a more appropriate descriptive title for "hair stylist".

6. 3 Diversity Requiring Tendencies of Mind

The world is changing dramatically and, as a result, people are more and more dissatisfied with the fixed patterns of the old society. They prefer the fresher and more attractive words or expressions. Therefore, a wide diversity of mental attitudes motivates the appearance of the new lexis to describe new products, and new events or phenomenon in a new society.

As for the categories of meaning-changed words, some may be taken in a linguistic style, some in types of word meaning, some from a grammatical and lexical point of view, and some with denotative and connotative meanings. No matter from which perspective, it has been observed by linguists and semanticists that the change of word-meaning follows a number of patterns, with the major ones being extension, narrowing, degradation, and elevation, according to the range of their usage and the attitude towards their senses.

6.4 Summary

As mentioned above, the way the new lexis is formed not only reflects man's physical activities but also mirrors the inner world of man's mind. Therefore, language study should be closely related to man's psychological process (桂诗春, 1991). Many new lexis stand for the concentrated form of different mental activities, as well as of many physical activities, of human beings. Man's mental activities, including his thinking patterns, in turn strongly affect the invention of new lexis. The interrelationship between the two could be better understood in the following illustrated in Figure 6-1.

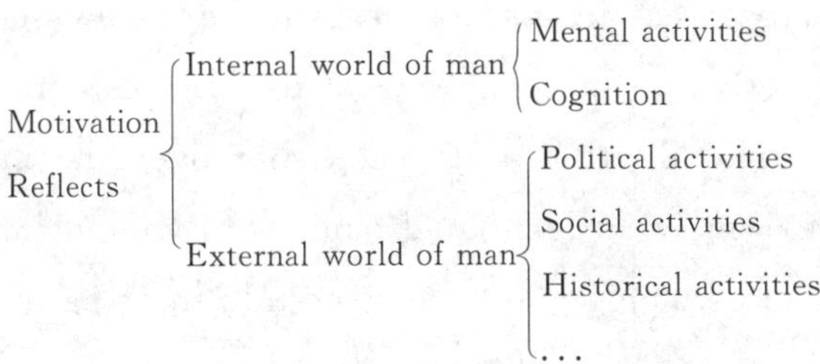

Figure 6-1 The worlds that lexical motivation reflects

No matter which motivation it belongs to, the changes they bring forward are all a reflection of man's activities. The newly formed words, as the carrier of cultures, and the pictures of man's activities, are sure to reflect man's mind and cognition.

Chapter Seven Etymological Motivations of New English Lexis

7.1 Etymology and Motivation

Etymology means something approximating to the paraphrase "original meaning, or use, of a given lexical unit or proper name". It studies the origin and history of a word, the changes of the form and meaning, including the borrowing words. Tracing back to a word's development shows that in many cases what are now separate lexical items were formerly one and the same word. The deep prehistory of our language has nurtured little word-seeds that over the millennia have proliferated into widely differentiated families of vocabulary.

The study of etymology can be divided into three parts: i, the origin of words and the meaning and form which can be traced back; ii, the motivation of the words, that is, the relationship between the original meaning and form of words; iii, the change of the form and meaning of words.

The life stories of individual words, often mazy and conjectural, need a fixed backdrop if they are to make sense. So first, a little history.

English is a member of the Indo-European family of languages. The precise origins of this are still a matter of some controversy, but the general view is that it came on the scene around 8,000 years ago in the general area to the north of the Black Sea. Since then it has split up into a large number of subgroups, which today provide nearly all the languages of Europe and have also spread over large areas of the Middle East and northern India.

But in the history of English, there are two particular groups that are of central importance. The first is the Romance languages: classical Latin, the literary language of ancient Rome; and French, Italian, Spanish, Portuguese, and Rumanian, which evolved from Vulgar Latin, the language of the common people that spread through the Western Roman Empire. The role of Latin and French, in particular, in the growth of English vocabulary has been immense. A sizable proportion of English words were acquired from one or other of these sources.

The second important group, of course, is the German languages: for that is the group which English itself belongs. The existence of the German peoples as a separate speech community dates back to at least 3,000 years, when they all spoke the same language. Around the 2nd century BC this began to split up into three distinct dialects. One was East German. The only east German language which any written evidence survives is Gothic. Now extinct, it was spoken by German peoples who migrated back eastwards to the area of modern Bulgaria and the Crimea. The second was north German, which has evolved into modern Swedish, Danish, Norwegian, and Icelandic. And lastly there was West German, the ancestor of modern German, Dutch, Flemish, and English.

It was around this time that English started to roam beyond its

historical boundaries. As English merchant adventurers sailed the world, not only did they take their language with them to distant continents, where it has since become in many cases the dominant form of speech, but they also brought back with them new and exotic terms that have found their way into the English lexicon. There is not a major language in the world that has not over the past 500 made some contribution to English, from Italian and Hindi to the more modest gifts from the likes of Finnish and Tibetan.

English is still growing. Over half of the new items come from combinations of old ones, but there continues to be a lot of borrowing from other languages (glasnost and perestroika are notable examples from the 1980s).

From the above we can see that the etymology of words can be traced back to native language and foreign languages. Within a native language, the etymological motivation often exists in history, culture and literature of a nation, while in foreign languages, it can be reflected in borrowing words.

Etymology and motivation are closely tied up with each other. But there are different opinions on the relations between etymology and motivation. Some linguists argue that motivation is a part of etymology. The second opinion is that motivation is equal to etymology or inner form of words. Chinese linguists Zhang Yong-yan said that the inner form introduced by Honbout was actually the etymology or motivation as a reason to express some idea by certain sounds; the purpose of such research was to explore why it got the very name or expression (Zhang, 1981). A third opinion is that motivation and etymology are two different concept belong to different field though they may be closely related to each other; the research of etymology is to explore the origins of words, while the research on motivation focuses on the background and hidden causes of words which is beyond etymology. In this book, we prefer the third opinion.

English etymology is regarded as boring, abstract and widely involved. Memorizing new words is seen as a time-consuming but sometimes fruitless task. But if we know the hidden stories of some English words, we'll find it easy to understand and memorize these words. In the following, we will focus on seven kinds of motivations of English new words as far as etymology is concerned. Here new words involve not only modern and fashionable English words, but also some old words with new meanings and interpretations.

7.2 Motivation of Words from Historical Events

Many English words can be traced back to historical events. The word "kangaroo" is a good case in point. It came from Australian. In fact it didn't refer to the local animal but meant "I don't know what you say". How was it created? In the 18th century, a famous English explorer and captain named James Cook (1728—1779) arrived at the continent and saw a peculiar animal which he had never seen before. So he asked the local people what the animal was. But the man didn't understand him, and replied "Kang-a-roo" which meant "I don't know what you say" in that language. Cook was very satisfied and wrote down the pronunciation and took it back to England. When other English people reached the Australia they were eager to see what "kangaroo" looked like. They asked the local people, but the local people seemed much confused. Up to then did they understand that Cook made a mistake. But the word "kangaroo" was thus created and used up to now.

Another example is "Dutch". In English, the word Dutch is related to something deteriorate. That is because in the 17th century, England and Dutch were two big business powers and they fought for the control over the sea. So the English people were quite hatred for the Dutchmen. As a result, "Dutch" is deteriorately used, such as in "go Dutch, do a Dutch(escape, suicide), double Dutch(words difficult to understand), in Dutch (be in trouble), talk Dutch (nonsense)" and so on.

In English, the word "Waterloo" can be used to indicate failure as in "meet one's Waterloo". The origin of that word lies in history. Waterloo is the name of a place where Napoleon was once defeated. Another example is Dunkirk, which means "be in difficulty". For example, we say "Dunkirk in foreign trade" which means a crisis in foreign trade. That is because in World War Ⅱ, the British Army was defeated and retreated from Dunkirk, a seaport in northern France.

"Freshman and sophomore" refer to first-year and second-year college student respectively. The two words can be traced back to about 1550BC. Since first-year college students, boys and girls, were lovely, pure and curious about new things, they became "freshmen". Sophomore originated from Greek: sophos means wise and moros means foolish. So the literal meaning of sophomore is the wise fool. It is regarded as students who look wise but actually quite innocent and ignorant.

"Burn one's boats" means doing something that make it impossible to go back to a previous situation. In 106BC—44BC, Julius Caesar the Emperor of the ancient Rome led his army to fight against other countries and always won the wars. The secret was that he had all of their own boats burned when fighting so that the soldiers had no way to retreat but two choices: to win or to die. That greatly encouraged the soldiers and they fought much more bravely for their own lives. People later used this event and created that phrase "to encourage oneself to go forward without retreat route."

7.3 Motivation of Words from Culture and Customs

Language is closely associated with culture. Some languages are difficult to understand without taking their culture and customs into consideration. Cultural motivation can be easily found in English words. Take the word "dangerous" for example. It is said that a long time ago, there was a wealthy and honored woman named Dangerous. She lived together illegally with a man named Damase, so she deserved the curse from the Bishop. One day while Damase was crossing a bridge, all of a sudden it rained and stormed. He was hit by the thunder and drowned himself. After his horrible death, Dangerous was so scared that she begged for pardon of the Bishop and lived the rest life alone. People then regarded her name as something hazard.

The word "*handkerchief*" is a compound word: hand+kerchief. In old French, kerchief referred to head-cover as decoration and protection. Later, people preferred to hold it in their hands. The word "handkerchief" was thus created.

The phrase "*go to Bath*" means "going away, idiot". Bath is located in the southwest of England which is famous for springs. Many patients with mental disease are sent there to recuperate. If someone asks you to go to Bath, it indicates that he hates to see you and asks you to go away immediately.

The phrase "*behind the eight ball*" is not easy to understand without

knowing the background culture. In the ball game pool, the player must hit 15 balls into the six pockets in the corners of the playing table in order. The 8th ball must be the last. If that ball is accidentally in the way, the player will get into the trouble and have difficulty in playing the game. If he hits that ball, he will lose some score. Life is just like the ball game. When we are in trouble or in misfortune, we often say "somehow I wind up behind the ball".

Another example is the "*Black Friday*". In the western countries, people usually call their unlucky day as "*Black Friday*" even though it is not Friday at all the day the misfortune occurs. The following two convincing explanations may account for the reasons:

Firstly, it is said on the Friday before the Easter, Jesus suffered distress and was killed. Later on Friday, priests were often dressed in black to honor Jesus. As a result, *Black Friday* was seen as unlucky day. Secondly, the reason why Friday was regarded as unlucky is that many disasters took place on Friday. For example, the notorious Great Depression took place on Friday, Sept. 13, 1873, when the stocks in New York Stock Exchange dropped dramatically and millions of millionaires became nothing-men. On the same day World War I broke out. Later on, western people regard misfortunate days as *Black Friday*.

Black sheep refers to those who are referred to as a disgrace or a failure by other members of his family or group. It is said that in ancient England, people regarded raising black sheep as a misfortune, because black wool was not as valuable as white wool, thus black sheep was viewed as something useless. Now a member of his family of group who is notorious for his deeds is called "black sheep". For example: His brother is a black sheep of the family. Poor Dick, he was the black of the company, always in disgrace.

Blackmail, from the literal form, you may think that it is a mail with black cover. But as a matter of fact, it has nothing to do with mail. In ancient Scotland, *mail* meant *land rent* (Now farmer who rents land is still called mailer). There were some local bandits who not only robbed farmers of private possessions but also forced them to contribute animals and crops, which were called blackmail. Gradually, it changed to mean "demanding money or things from others by illegal forces or threatening to reveal information which could harm him".

The phrase "*face the music*" is easily to be misunderstood if you don't know its cultural origins. If someone says "I'll have to go to face the music", you should not mistake it as "he is going to the concert". Instead, it means facing and experiencing difficulty or reaping the bitter fruit one has sown. According to American novelist James Fenimore Cooper, the first one who used that phrase were those actors who waited near the stage for their turn to perform. They just faced the orchestra when they were on the stage, and even forgot the lines with nervousness for fear of being taunted. So they often said to themselves to focus their attentions on, "It's time to go to face the music." Another explanation is that in American army, if a soldier behaved badly and was forced to leave the army and went through the shame, the band would not play music, but beat a drum slowly. Thus the phrase developed the meaning of "be responsible for one's evil behavior". For example: After he was caught with the stolen goods, he had to *face the music*.

Take French leave now means "creep silently without saying good-bye or to leave one's work or duty without obtaining permission". "To take leave" means "to say goodbye or go away". It is widely acknowledged that it is good manners to say good-bye before leaving. So from the phrase it seemed that French people were quite rude and

impolite. Actually, this phrase stems from an interesting story. According to C. T. Onions' *The Shorted Oxford English Dictionary* (1955), in the 17th century in France, it was widely accepted that guests invited to a party need not say good-bye to the host or hostess before leaving. English people regarded it as impolite and called it "take French leave". Of course, that annoyed French people and they made a revenge on them by creating another French phrase "filer a'l' anglaise", in English which means "to go off in English style". We should note that the phrase is used in informal way. For example: He took a French leave and showed a clean pair of heels.

7.4 Motivation of Words from Literature

Literature is the products of language, in return, language is greatly ripened with the prosperity of literature. We can find that many English words are derived from literature motivation.

For example, the phrase "Aladdin's lamp" originates from the famous Arabian fairy tale "The Thousand and One Nights". The hero Aladdin was cheated by an evil witch into getting a lamp which could bring everything the owner wanted. Without the lamp, everything would disappear. So Aladdin's lamp is used to refer to any "magic weapon which can make people's dream come true".

May-December is another example. At first glance, the phrase has nothing to do with love or marriage. As a matter of fact, it is metaphorically used as "marriage of a young lady with an old man or a young man with an old lady". Geoffrey Chaucer was a famous ancient British poet. In his masterpiece *Canterbury Tales*, there was a story about a young lady named May who was married to an elder gentleman named January. Gradually somehow Chaucer's May and January changed into May and December. The following example is a good case which appeared in *New York Times* in September, 1991: When Charlie Chaplin married Oona O'neil in 1943, he was 54 and she was 18. The *May-December* marriage so infuriated the father of the bride, famous playwright Eugene O'neill, that he disinherited her.

The phrase "make my day" means "make me very happy". According to Robert Hendrickson's "Encyclopedia of Etymology", the phrase originated from the famous American female writer Florence Barclay' novel "The Rosary". The original sentence is as follows: I knew I wanted her; knew her presence *made my day* and her absence meant chill night. Now that phrase is often present in newspapers and magazines. For example, in Washington Post of May, 1990, it read: Watching women, sharing his impression of how they look, "*makes my day*," he says. In the film *Sudden Impact*, the policeman Harry challenged the scoundrel: Go ahead, *make my day*! It means: if you make force, I will kill you with one shot. That will be a meaningful day for me.

"The Little Engine That Could" is a household name even to American children written by Watty Piper in 1930. The story is about an obscure train engine offered to carry a large group of children to the destination and overcame remarkable difficulties on the way. Thus the little engine became the hero. So this well-known idiom now means "nothing in the world is difficult for one who sets his heart on it". For example, American State Railway named Amtrak was often criticized by the public for its poor operation and management even after the high-speed train named ACELA was put into practice in 2002. So someone laughed at it, "Amtrak may have to change the name of its premier high-speed ACELA trains to The Little Engine That Couldn't (Hartford

Courant, 8/20/2002)".

The phrase "*sour grapes*" originated from the famous *Aesop's Fables*, which means someone is keen to get something but can't obtain it, so he comforts himself by pretending to show no interest in it and even devalue it. The well-known fable named "The Fox and the Grapes" is of great significance and is used as a text in many countries. It reads: once upon a time a fox was very hungry and thirsty and eagerly looking for something to eat. He looked up when he saw many ripe grapes hanging attractively on the high trellis. Unfortunately, he could not reach the grapes as he could not climb so high. So he could do nothing but jumped up and down in vain. At last, green-eyed, though, he said to himself, "The grapes are sour, and not at all fit for my eating." Thus, the phrase "sour grapes" is to describe people who pretends to believe that what he cannot have is of little value or importance. For example: But because we cannot satisfy the desires of our hearts—why should we cry "sour grapes" at them? (H. Wells, *Christina Alberta's Father*, book III, ch. III. 5)

"An ugly duckling" is derived from *Antosen's Fairy Tales*. It refers to a person who at first seems unpromising but who later becomes much admired, very able, etc. A mother duck hatched a big and extremely ugly duckling. He was so ugly that it seemed the whole world didn't welcome his coming to the world. Upon his birth he was hit, pushed out, and looked down upon. There was no room for him on such a large world. But he did not give in, instead he flied bravely in the cold sky to get rid of the unfairness. At last the miracle occurred that he grew into a remarkably beautiful swan! Now the phrase refers to those insignificant people who were once looked down upon. For example: Susan was the ugly duckling in her family, until she grew up.

7.5 Motivations of Words from Greek Gods

Greek culture made a dramatic effect on English words. Many English words are derived from Greek mythology. Now these words are still widely used and have been added to new meanings.

Zeus and jovial

In Greek myths, immortals governed the earth and heaven. *Zeus* was the leader of gods. He, together with his followers, lived in Mount Olympus. In Roman myths, Zeus was called *Jove* or *Jupiter*. Now in English, *Jove* means "My god". The largest planet was named after *Jupiter* to indicate its large size. Astrologists believe that people born in the months of Jupiter are happy and joyful. So the word *jovial* (the adjective form of jove) means "happy, joyful". For example, a jovial old fellow.

Perfect Apollo

The sun God Apollo was the son of Zeus. He was in charge of brightness, youth, hunting, music and poems. He was a versatile, good-mannered, handsome young man and was very popular to the world. So if a man is called a perfect Apollo, he is seen as a standard handsome man with perfect manners.

Muse and music

Muses, the daughters of Zeus, were nine goddesses who were in charge of music, poetry, dancing, history and other branches of art and literature. They were young and beautiful and energetic. So the word *muse* means spirit that inspires a creative artist, especially a poet. The words music and museum originated from Muses. People say "Muses like peace and hate wars", which means wars of conflicts do harm to the

progress of art or literature.

Psyche and soul

The love story between love god Eros and Psyche is one of the most touching comics in Greek legends. Psyche was a pretty beautiful princess. Her beauty aroused the envy of Aphrodite (Venus in Roman myths). She ordered her son Eros to make Psyche fall in love with the ugliest man on the world. But Eros could not help loving Psyche. His mother was so angry that she tortured Psyche. At last the lovers got married after experiencing great suffers and difficulties. In western world, Psyche is the symbol of one's soul and spirit. She is pictured as a young girl with wings of butterfly. The word psychic is now concerned with processes and soul and mind. Psychic research is the study and investigation of psychical phenomena. The prefix *psycho-* is related to mind, such as psychology, psychoanalyst, psychotherapy.

Cupid

Eros or Cupid, was the primal god of Love; using arrows of gold and lead, he would wound the hearts of mortals and immortals alike. Cupid is the son of Hephaestus, the smith-god and Venus, the love-goddess. He fired the arrow which caused Helen of Troy to fall in love with Aphrodite's young ward, the Trojan Prince Paris, but he did balk at forcing the Phoenician princess Psyche to fall in love with a mortal beyond her dignity. Scratching himself on one of his own arrows, he fell in love with Psyche himself and spirited her off to live in secrecy with her. Now Cupid is regard as the symbol of love. If someone falls in love, we often say "he is hit by Cupid's arrows".

Prometheus and Pandora's Box

In Greek mythology, Pandora ("all gifted") was the first woman, fashioned by Zeus as part of the punishment of mankind for Prometheus' theft of the secret of fire. Pandora was the first woman on earth. Zeus ordered Hephaestus, the god of craftsmanship, to create a woman and he did, using water and earth. The gods endowed her with many talents; Aphrodite gave her beauty, Apollo music, Hermes persuasion, and so forth. Hence her name: Pandora, "all-gifted". When Prometheus stole fire from heaven, Zeus took vengeance by presenting Pandora to Epimetheus, Prometheus' brother. With her, Pandora had a jar which she was not to open under any circumstance. Impelled by her natural curiosity, Pandora opened the jar, and all evil contained escaped and spread over the earth. She hastened to close the lid, but the whole contents of the jar had escaped, except for one thing which lay at the bottom, and that was Hope. Now in modern English, the Pandora's Box metaphor is powerful both in its imagery and its suggestiveness. Pandora's Box does not label only the magical present given by Zeus to Pandora, which contained all human evils, but relates to all sources of unexpected extensive troubles.

Herculean Task

Today, the phrase *Herculean Task* refers to a difficult chore. The term arose from the ancient stories of Hercules.

Hercules is the Roman name for the Greek mythological hero Heracles (sometimes Herakles), who was famous for his courage and strength. He was the illegal son of Zeus. Zeus's wife, Hera, was duly angered over the impending birth of Hercules. She succeeded in delaying his birth, but her attempt to kill him by sending two snakes into his crib failed—Hercules strangled both of them. The many feats of Hercules are customarily divided into the 12 labors and other exploits. He worked through 12 labors, which were performed for the Greek king Eurystheus as a result of Hera's enmity. Among Greek and Roman philosophers,

Hercules was considered a hero-saint, the epitome of one who chose virtue over pleasure and endured a hard life on earth to enjoy immortality with the gods.

Ceres and cereal

Ceres was Zeus' sister. She was goddess of the cornfield, mistress of planting and harvesting. Her daughter, Persephone, was raised among flowers and looked like a flower herself. One day, Persephone was kidnapped by Hades, god of the underworld or hell. Ceres went home to look for her daughter, but since then, nothing grew on field. Trees were stripped of leave. The soil was hard and cracked. The people were starving. Zeus was concerned about the world and pronounced his judgment that Persephone had to spend six months each year with her mother and six months with Hades in the underworld. That is why summer and winter are the way they are. That is why there is a time for planting, and a time when the earth must rest in winter. Besides, the word *cereal* thus came into being from goddess Ceres.

7.6 Motivations of Words from the *Bible*

In the western world, the *Bible* has been making a considerable influence on language. Many English words are rooted from that well-known work.

Adam's apple refers to man's pharynx in his throat. According to the *Bible*, Adam and Eve who lived in the Eden, were prohibited by the God from eating the apples on the wisdom tree. But Eve, lured by the evil snake Sadan, ate an apple and also gave one to Adam. Just then the God appeared angrily and it was too late for Adam to swallow the apple. So the apple stuck in his throat and became "Adam's apple".

Handwriting on the wall has nothing to do with words on the wall. Actually, it refers to somebody who is doomed to fail and his number is up. According to the *Bible*, the King Belshazzar enjoyed the big party in his palace when a mysterious hand sprang up and wrote down four mysterious words on the wall. A predictor Daniel told the king that the handwriting on the wall indicated the king was in danger. Soon, it came true. The king was killed in a war. So the phase now means *ill omen*.

7.7 Motivations of Words from Names of People and Places

A few English words come from the names of people and places.

Coffee stems from the names of place where it was originally planted. The story of how coffee growing and drinking spread around the world is one of the greatest and most romantic in history. It starts in the Horn of Africa, in Ethiopia, where the coffee tree probably originated in the province of Kaffa. There are various fanciful but unlikely stories surrounding the discovery of the properties of roasted coffee beans. One story has it that about 1,000 years ago, a goatherd in Ethiopia's south-western highlands plucked a few red berries from some young green trees growing there in the forest and tasted them. He liked the flavour—and the feel-good effect followed. Today those self-same berries, dried, roasted and ground, have become the world's second most popular non-alcoholic beverage after tea. And, as David Beatty discovers in words and pictures, the Ethiopian province where they first blossomed—Kaffa—gave its name to coffee. The stimulant became fashionable throughout Europe. By the late seventeenth century, the drink was enjoyed under numerous names—English *coffee*, French and Spanish

café, German *koffee*.

In 1820 German chemist F. Runge extracted a stimulus from coffee seeds and called it *Caffeine*.

Real McCoy, American slang, means the real thing or the ultimate experience of achievement.

Its origin is unclear but there is broad agreement among a lot of writers that it originated from the name of the American boxer Norman Selby, known as Kid McCoy, who was welterweight champion from 1898—1900. It is said that McCoy had so many imitators who took his name in boxing booths in small towns throughout the country that eventually he had to bill himself as Kid "The Real" McCoy, and the phrase stuck. There's another anecdote in which a skeptical drunk who met the boxer in a bar denied he was the real boxer with such force that McCoy was forced to hit him. After recovering the drunk said, "It's the real McCoy!"

The word *sandwich* for an item of food that we use today was born in London during the very late hours one night in 1762 when an English nobleman, John Montagu, the Fourth Earl of Sandwich (1718—1792), was too busy gambling to stop for a meal even though he was hungry for some food. The legend goes that he ordered a waiter to bring him roast-beef between two slices of bread. The Earl was able to continue his gambling while eating his snack; and from that incident, we have inherited that quick-food product that we now know as the *sandwich*.

7.8 Motivations of Borrowing Words

Adopted and borrowed words enrich the English words. Most English words have been imported from elsewhere, either when invasions of England took place (e.g., the Romans, the Vikings and the Normans) or when the English invaded other countries (e.g., America and India). Imports from Greek, Latin, Norse, French, German, Spanish Italian and Dutch are so numerous as to be unremarkable. Here are some of the examples:

Greek: atom, electricity, obstetrics

Latin: tumor, cancer, i.e., e.g., etc.

French: entail, cafe, extraordinaire

Chinese: tea, kung-fu, koutou

Japanese: kimono, jodo

Borrowing words can be done directly or indirectly. For example, the word "feast" was borrowed directly from French "festa", and the word "algebra" was borrowed indirectly from Arabic through Spanish. Many English words of Greek origin are borrowed via Latin or French.

There are several types of borrowing words of English.

Loanwords: Both form and meaning are borrowed with only a slight adaptation to the phonological system of the new language. For instance, English borrowed "au pair"(who receives board and lodging with a family in return for helping with the housework), "coup d'etat" (blows that kills a person or destroy his hope) from French.

Loanblend: Part of the form is native and part is borrowed, while the meaning is fully borrowed. For example, the first part of the word "coconut" was from Spanish, while the second part originated from English.

Loanshift: the meaning is borrowed, while the form is native. For instance, "bridge" is an English word, but it also means a type of card game which borrowed from the Italian "ponte".

Loan Translation: it is a special type of borrowing, in which each morpheme or word is translated into the literal equivalent morpheme or word in another language. For example, "paper tiger" and "running dog" come from a Chinese expression. "Black humor" is a loan translation from French "humor noir", etc.

7.9 Summary

Etymological motivation of new English words is related to a lot of social-cultural factors, but the origin of words is not easily found in many cases and the meaning concerned with etymological motivation can not be obtained literally. Some words have lost their etymological motivation with the change of language.

Second, in English loan words from Indo-European languages, such as Greek and French, have higher motivation than those borrowed from other languages.

Third, the above mentioned seven sources fully show the origin of English words and the motivation. But there may be more sources of the origin of the motivation and we hope that it will be more convincing with further research in that field.

Chapter Eight The L2 Mental Lexicon and Lexis Acquisition

The development of a rich vocabulary is an important element in acquisition of a second language (Nunan, 1991). Aitchison (1987) claimed that the number of words known by an educated adult is unlikely to be less than 50,000 and may be as high as 250,000. And each word involves its various word knowledge including phonological, orthographic, syntactic, morphological and semantic aspects. All these information are stored in the mental lexicon which is an absolutely complex structure. Despite its complexity and richness, however, these various aspects of word knowledge and words have not prevented people from getting access to and retrieving words efficiently because words and word knowledge are supposed to be organized in the mental lexicon in a systematic way for both fast comprehension and easy production. One of Aitchison' s experiments indicated that native speakers (NS) can recognize a word in 200 milliseconds or less from its onset, which confirmed the assumption that the mental lexicon must be well organized. Therefore, knowing the structure of the mental lexicon is very important in the teaching and learning of vocabulary.

To the mental lexicon, people have been curious about its structure

and presented a lot of assumptions: It could be organized by phonological similarity, such as the words which start with the same letter (banana, beer, book, big, beak) or end with the same phoneme (look, sleek, pike, black and so on), by semantic similarity, such as banana, apple, pear, orange and so on, by orthography, by frequency of use, etc.

To explore the nature of the mental lexicon, researchers used several research tools such as slips of the tongue, error analysis, word association (WA) tests, malapropisms and introspection. Among them, WA tests have been regarded as an effective way to explore the nature of mental lexicon. The use of WA tests in first language psychological research has a long history but has only fairly recently been employed in L2 lexical studies (Zareva, 2007). More recently, WA tests have been widely used to collect information about the organization and development of the mental lexicon as well as to examine the mental state of individual subjects, their cognitive abilities and social attitudes.

8.1 The Notion of Mental Lexicon

The study of the mental lexicon can be traced back to the late 1960s. Treisman (1960) first proposed the concept of mental lexicon. According to him, a mental lexicon is normally defined as a repository of all the information a reader or listener has attained about the words of his language. He suggested that in every speaker's mind there is a well-organized system of lexical representation, where each word's spelling (orthography), sound (phonology) and meaning (semantics) are assumed to be stored as unique entities. Similarly, Richards and Schmidt (2002) defined a mental lexicon as a mental system that contains all the information a person knows about words. These properties include the meaning of the word, its spelling and pronunciation, its relationship to other words, and related information. Some scholars (e.g., Aitcheson, 2003; Channel, 1988; McCarthy, 1990) have used metaphors to define the mental lexicon. McCarthy (1990) has likened the mental lexicon to a dictionary, a thesaurus, an encyclopedia, a library, a computer, or a net. The information in the mental lexicon is always being updated. New words are added, new connections to existing words are made and unused words may be forgotten.

8.2 The Internal Structure of the Lexical Entries

Every entry must convey certain information despite where it exists. A lexical entry in L1 learner's mind is generally considered to contain semantic, syntactic, morphological and formal (phonological and orthographic) specifications about a lexical item (Carroll, 2000). It is believed that these different types of information are represented in the two components that make up a lexical entry: the lemma and the lexeme. (Levelt, 1989) The lemma contains semantic and syntactic information about a word (for instance, word meaning and part of speech) while the lexeme contains morphological and formal information (for example, different morphological variants of a word, spelling and pronunciation). Figure 8-1 provides a graphic description of a lexical entry (see Figure 8-1).

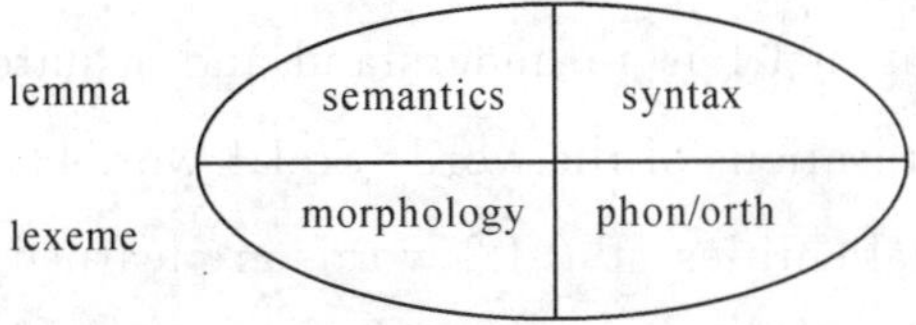

Figure 8-1 The internal structure of the lexical entry (adapted from Levelt, 1989)

An important feature of the lexical representation in L1 is that these

different types of information are integrated within each entry. Once the entry is opened, all the information automatically becomes available. It was found that phonological information is automatically activated in visual word recognition (Van Orden, 1987; Perfette et al, 1988) even in languages such as Chinese where phonological information is unlikely to assist visual word recognition (Perfetti & Zhang, 1995). Further evidence comes from the finding that both meanings of an ambiguous word are initially activated even when sentential context clearly favors one of the meanings (Swinney, 1979). The integration of different kinds of semantics, morphology, syntax, phonology and orthography information into lexical entries is not acquired easily. It requires an extensive, highly contextualized exposure to the language. With such highly contextualized input, an L1 learner is able to extract the semantic, syntactic and morphological information of the word easily

Based on the internal structure of the lexical entry model put forward by Levelt, Jiang (2000) proposes a more acceptable supposition for the representation of lexical entries in the L2 mental lexical, which distinguishes three stages of L2 lexical development on the basis of the information represented in the lexical entry.

At the first stage, which is known as the formal stage, a lexical entry is established for an L2 lexical word, but it only contains its formal specifications. Little content is established within the entry. The task of lexical development in L1 is to understand and acquire the meaning as well as other specifications of the word. So L1 words are learned as both semantic and formal entities. But L2 words are learned mainly as formal entities because the meaning is provided either through association with L1 translation or by means of definition. An L2 word is hardly learned from the context by the learner himself. The learner's attention is focused on the formal entities of the word, i. e. spelling and pronunciation. Therefore, a lexical entry in L2 initially only contains its formal specifications within the lexical entry. It may also contain a pointer that directs attention to the L1 translation equivalent. This pointer serves as a link between L2 words and their counterparts in L1. L2 lexical items at the initial stage can be considered as lexical items without lemmas, or the lemma structure is empty. Figure 8-2 provides a description of this stage. Following the distinction of lemma and lexeme as two components of a lexical entry, L2 lexical items at the initial state can be considered lexical items without lemmas, or the structure is empty (De Bot et al, 1997).

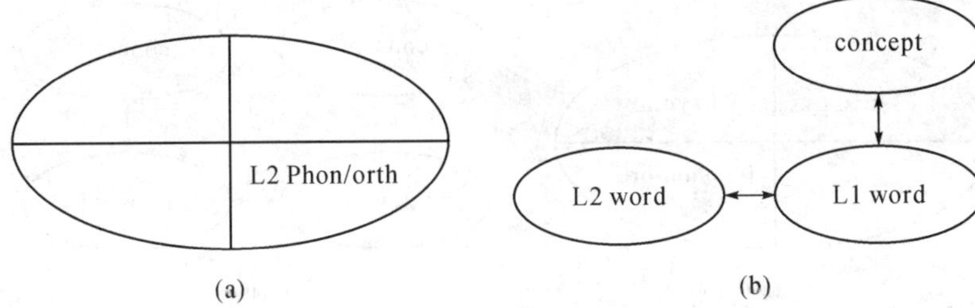

Figure 8-2 The first stage (adapted from Jiang, 2000)

Although little content is established within the entry, the semantic, syntactic and morphological information may also be available to learners. Learners may learn such information through the activation of L1-L2 links. They may also have learned some explicit grammatical rules about these words. Under both circumstances, however, such semantic and grammatical information is not an integrative part of L2 mental lexicon. In other words, it cannot be retrieved automatically in the communication, and then in this case, it is part of learners' lexical knowledge, not learners' lexical competence.

The second stage is called the L1 lemma mediation stage. At this

stage, stronger associations are developed between L2 words and their L1 translations. What these strong associations mean, among other things, is the simultaneous activation of L2 word forms and the lemma information (semantic and syntactic specifications) of L1 counterparts in L2 word use. The repeated simultaneous activation of L2 lexical forms and L1 lemma suggests that L1 lemma information (semantic and syntactic information) may be copied to L2 lexical forms. This stage is called the L1 lemma mediation stage because the lemma space of an L2 word is occupied by the lemma information from its L1 translation equivalents and the L1 lemma information mediates L2 word processing. Figure 8-3 depicts a lexical entry at this stage.

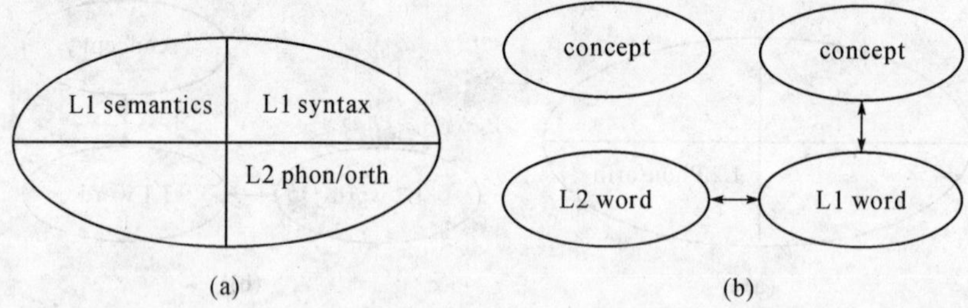

Figure 8-3 The second stage (adapted from Jiang, 2000)

The third stage is called the L2 integration stage. If his lexical competence in L2 is developed fully, a learner can extract from context all the specifications of an L2 word. At this stage, the semantic, syntactic and morphological specifications of an L2 word are extracted from exposure and use and integrated into the lexical entry. At this stage, a lexical entry in L2 will be similar to a lexical entry in L1 (see Figure 8-4).

Thus, lexical development in L2 can, now, be seen as comprising three stages, as shown in Figure 8-4. At the formal stage of lexical development, a lexical entry is established in the L2 lexicon, but it

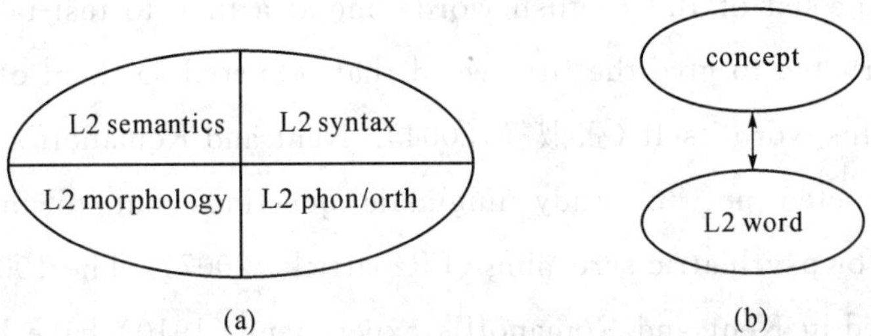

Figure 8-4 The third stage (adapted from Jiang, 2000)

contains only formal specifications and a pointer. As a learner's experience in the language increases, semantic and syntactic information of an L2 word's L1 translation equivalent may be copied or attached to the entry of an L2 word to form lexical entries that consist of L2 forms and L1 lemmas. At the final stage, semantic, syntactic, morphological, as well as formal specifications about an L2 word are established within the lexical entry. In this way, words are in transition from one stage to another.

These representational feature lead to two essential processing consequences: (1) A higher degree of automatic activation in L2 production is achieved as a result of the direct connection between L2 lexical forms and L1 lemma information. (2) The selection of morphological forms becomes a conscious process.

8.3 The Notion of Word Association (WA) Tests

The WA test was initially used as a psychological tool to study the subconscious mind. It was invented by Francis Galeton, a British scientist, who tested himself and published his results in 1879. This provided an inspiration for other WA tests in the late 1880s. The first large-scale WA test was performed by Kent and Romanoff (1910), who

read aloud a list of 100 English words one at a time to test-takers who were instructed to give the first word that occurred to them other than the stimulus word itself (张淑静,2004). Kent and Romanoff's WA test was conducted not to study linguistic questions but to investigate methods for psychiatric screening (Fitzpatrick, 2007). The 100 English words used in Kent and Romanoff's experiment (1910) have become a norm list and been used in further association studies for both children and adults.

More recently, WA tests have been used by psycholinguists to explore the mental lexicon. Most mental lexicon research is driven by the belief that association behavior can reveal information about the development and organization of the mental lexicon. As Aitcheson (2003) claimed, an analysis of the responses to a stimulus word may give useful information about how words might be linked together in a person's mind. It has been widely believed that WA tests can reveal information about the development and organization of the mental lexicon.

In the early 1960s and 1970s, WA tests were applied to L1 mental lexicon and the bilingual mental lexicon study. The last few decades saw the application of WA tests in the L2 mental lexicon study.

There are different kinds of WA tests: Free WA tests, discrete WA tests and continuous WA tests (Dong, 1998). In free WA tests subjects are required to generate responses of any types, in discrete WA tests they are required to give only one response per stimulus and in continuous WA tests they are asked to produce as many WAs as possible to each stimulus of a set within a pre-specified time limit (Li, 2004).

Although WA tests have different procedures, the underlying principle remains the same: Stimulus words are presented to the subject (either verbally or in written form) and then the subjects are asked to respond with the first word or words that come to mind or they are encouraged to produce as many associates as possible per stimulus word within a given time span. The last part of the test is to classify and analyze the responses.

8.4 Traditional Classifications of Association Responses

Word associations are typically classified as phonological or semantic. The semantic association can be subdivided into paradigmatic and systematic responses. Paradigmatic responses usually refer to words from the same grammatical class and a similar semantic area. By contrast, systematic responses usually belong to different grammatical categories and the stimulus words and can co-occur in grammatically well-formed expressions. In other words, they form a clear sequential or collocation relation with the stimulus words. Phonological responses, also known as *clang* associations, are phonologically related to the stimulus words.

The specific classifications are as follows.

1) Paradigmatic responses: coordinates, ordinates, synonyms or antonyms.

a) Synonyms are words which have different forms but similar meanings.

Dialectal synonyms—*lift/elevator*, *flat/apartment*

Synonyms of different styles—*gentleman/guy*

Synonyms of different registers—*salt/sodium chloride*

Synonyms differing in affective meaning—*attract/seduce*

Synonyms differing in collocation—*beautiful/handsome*, *able/capable*

b) Antonyms: A response is categorized as an antonym if it is opposite in meaning to the stimulus word (e.g., nervous—relaxed). There are several kinds of antonyms.

Gradable antonyms—pairs of words opposite to each other, but the positive of one word does not necessarily imply the negative of the other. For example, the word *hot* and *cold* are a pair of antonyms, but *not hot* does not necessarily mean *cold*, maybe *warm*, *mild* or *cool*. Therefore, this pair of antonyms is a pair of gradable antonyms.

Complementary antonyms-words opposite to each other and the positive of one implies the negative of the other (e.g., *alive/dead*).

Reversal (relational) antonyms-words that denote the same relation or process from one or the other direction (e.g., *Push/pull*, *up/down*, *teacher/student*).

c) Subordinates: A response is classified as a subordinate to the stimulus word if it is a specific term of the stimulus word (e.g., fruit-apple, human-men).

d) Super ordinates: A response is classified as a super ordinate to the stimulus word if it is an upper term or general term of the stimulus word (e.g., green-color, fruit-food).

e) Coordinates: A response is categorized as a coordinate to the stimulus word if it clusters together with the stimulus word on the same level of detail (e.g., salt-pepper, red-white) (Aitchison, 2003).

2) Systematic responses: two types of systematic relations are involved.

a) Sequential relations (e.g., nervous-very, concentrate-on).

b) Collocations, that is, syntagmatic relations between lexical items that have acquired such a high degree of idiomatic that the relationship does not follow from the meanings of the said items (e.g., school-a school of fish).

3) Clang responses: Some typical examples of clang associates are rhyming responses, responses with the same initial sounds as the stimulus or a similar consonant cluster (e.g., cherish-*finish*, wealth-*health*). In addition, clang associations also include nonsense words which cannot be classified into any other category.

8.5 Organization of L1 Mental Lexicon

8.5.1 Phonological Network vs. Semantic Network

The analysis of the slips of the tongue phenomena seems to indicate that words in the mental lexicon are related phonologically. TOT (tip-of-the-tongue) phenomena happen when we are not quite successful at retrieving a particular word but can usually remember something about how it sounds. Brown and McNeil found that people tended to confuse words with phonologically similar beginnings and endings. For example, when asked to produce the required low-frequency word "secant" after it was presented with its definitions, subjects were inclined to retrieve similar-sounding words such as "sexant" in the TOT state. Carroll (2000), in his discussion of the phonological knowledge, pointed out that people sometimes activate words by their sounds, which usually leads to speech errors of similar-sounding word substitution.

There are many examples. For instance, "Because I've got an apartment (*appointment*), they have been married (*measured*)." Garman (1990) George Bush said, "I don't want to run the risk of

ruining what is a lovely recession (*reception*)". (Newsweek, 1992, cited in Carroll, 2000) Brown and McNeil (1966) did an experiment in which they asked the subjects to name "A navigational instrument used measuring angular distances, especially the altitude of the sun, moon and stars at sea". When trying to get the word *sextant*, the subjects came up with *secant*, *sextet* and *sexton*, all of which obviously resembled the target, *sextant* (张淑静, 2004). In our daily life, there are also many examples like seventy (*seventeen*), Auckland (*Oakland*) and the question "did you get up late?" (*Did you get a plate*?)

However, there is some evidence from psycholinguistic studies in L1 that a native speaker's mental dictionary is not organized mainly on phonological links. Freedman and Loftus's study (1971) offered evidence. They asked the subjects to name a fruit that begins with letter *p* and name a word beginning with *p* that is a fruit respectively. The result showed that the subjects finished the former task more quickly than the latter. It seems to prove that semantically related items are stored together; therefore, it is more convenient for the subjects to extract them. According to Aitchison's finding (1987), the words in the same semantic field tend to be stored together, while words in different semantic fields are loosely related. Studies of malapropisms in native speakers' output also show evidence that the L1 lexicon must be arranged both semantically and phonologically (Fay and Cutler, 1977). The results of more recent studies conducted by Welter (2001) and Fitzpatrick (2006) also revealed that native speakers tend to respond with clang associates when presented with unfamiliar words. The items which triggered the most clang associations in Mara's experiment were also found to be the most difficult words.

All the findings confirm Fay and Cutler's (1977) assumption that there is one mental lexicon, phonologically and semantically arranged. In other words, the semantic network is so arranged that it is convenient for production, with words from the same semantic field linked closely. The phonological network is so arranged that it is convenient for fast identification of sounds in speech comprehension, with words which sound similar tightly bonded together (Aitchison, 1987).

These findings provide a basis for studies of the WA of language learners. L2 WA studies, to a large extent, followed L1 approaches to data collection and analysis.

8.5.2 The Hierarchical Network Model

The hierarchical network model is one of the important models of semantic network. It was put forward by Collins and Quillian (1969). It assumes that 'information might be stored just once and at the highest possible level for cognitive economy. The words are stored up in the memory in the form of networks, in which every word or concept is represented by a node and the relations between different nodes constitute a hierarchy. Some nodes are at the same level as other nodes, but meanwhile they belong to certain super-ordinate nodes or are themselves the super-ordinate nodes of other subordinate nodes. Thus their semantic features in this hierarchical network connect all the words with one another. According to this model, if several words share a certain semantic feature, then this shared feature must be stored at a super-ordinate node on the principle of cognitive economy. Namely, all the concepts are stored hierarchically in the mental lexicon. Different kinds of property relations are represented within a hierarchy. The concepts that are closely situated on the hierarchy would activate each other quickly.

In this model, it is assumed that the node representing animal stands higher than those two representing bird and fish. Similarly, bird stands higher than cannery and ostrich and fish higher than shark and salmon. The retrieval of concepts at the same level like "shark" and "salmon" is assumed to require same period of time while those at different levels requires different amount of time. However, in actual use, the time required for retrieval of "shark" and "salmon" is more likely to be influenced by each word's frequency. Therefore, the assumption that concepts at any given level are retrieved in an equal speed is wrong. And later researches suggest that this strict hierarchical model is not a good candidate for a model of mental lexicon.

8.5.3 The Spreading Activation Model

Although later researchers are not in support of the hierarchical network model, the notion of cognitive economy and networks has largely been retained. For example, as a revised network model, the spreading activation model (SAM) put forward by Collins and Loftus (1975) maintains the idea of a network. Words are represented in the mental lexicon in a network, yet the organization is not strictly hierarchical, but of a web structure. In this model, the mental lexicon is organized as a network of interconnected elements. The elements are concepts or nodes, which are connected to one another. The distances between different nodes are at once determined by structural property and functional factors. The intensity of relationship between different words is variable, according to various factors. In this model, all related concepts are linked through association. Therefore, the activation of one node may spread in different directions and even to the entire network.

Compared with the hierarchical network model, the spreading

activation model better displays complexity of organization of the mental lexicon. But it still fails to show us how complex the network really is. Both the hierarchical model and the spreading activation model are models of concepts, rather than models of words from the mental lexicon. This is because they do not take into account other dimensions of word knowledge but semantics, i.e. , the word's phonological, morphological or syntactic properties

8. 5. 4 The Extended Network Model

Based on the two models mentioned above, Bock and Levelt (945-84) put forward the extended network model (see Figure 8-5) in which

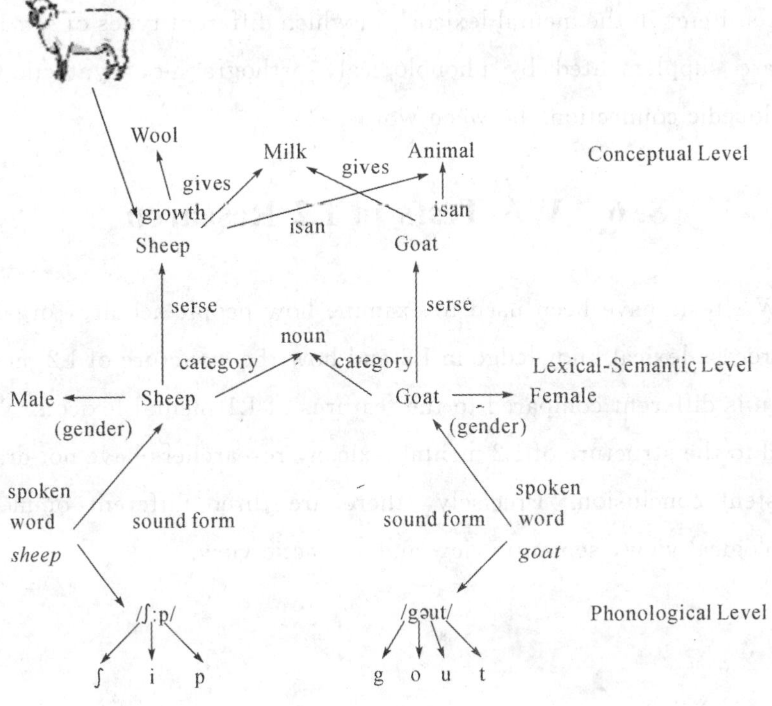

Figure 8-5 The extended network model (Bock and Levelt, 1945)

lexical knowledge involves three kinds of knowledge—conceptual level, lemma and lexeme. The conceptual level is similar to that of the spreading activation proposed by Collins and Loftus (1975), with nodes interconnected with each other by divergent relations and accessing degree. Lemma level refers to all the semantic and syntactic aspects of lexical knowledge, with all the syntactic and semantic properties included in it. The lexeme level refers to all the phonological and orthographic features of the lexical items. This model serves as a strong theoretical foundation for L2 lexical development and it is generally believed to be the relatively realistic and appealing one up till now because of its great similarity to the working process of human mind. This model tries to capture the multiple levels of interconnections between items in the mental lexicon, in which different types of semantic link are supplemented by phonological, orthographic, syntactic and encyclopedic connections between words.

8.6 WA Tests in L2 Research

WA tests have been used to examine how people acquire, organize and process lexical knowledge in L2 and how the structure of L2 mental lexicon is different compared to the features of L1 mental lexicon. With regard to the structure of L2 mental lexicon, researchers have not drawn consistent conclusion. Precisely, there are three different opinions: phonological view, semantic view and syntactic view.

8.7 Organization of L2 Mental Lexicon

8.7.1 Phonological View

The phonological view holds that the basis of the operations of the L2 mental lexicon is phonological rather than semantic, that "while in the native speaker's mental lexicon there are strong semantic links between words, the connections between words in additional languages are primarily phonological" (Laufer, 1989; Fromkin, 1971; Soudek, 1982). The most extensive study of L2 associative responses was conducted by Paul Mara, who was in charge of the Bareback Vocabulary Project at the University of London. Mara (1978) examined a group of 75 English learners of French. An analysis of students' responses revealed a high proportion of paradigmatic responses, few systematic responses and a very large number of clang associations. Most of the responses that appeared to be native-like could as well have been translations of English primary responses. Based on these findings, Mara concluded that there is a difference between the structure of the mental lexicon in native speakers and that of L2 learners: (1) The connections between words in the L2 learners' mental lexicon are less stable than the connections in the L1 mental lexicon; (2) Phonology appears to play a much more prominent organizing role in the L2 mental lexicon than it does in the L1 mental lexicon; (3) The semantic links between words tend to differ in a systematic way from those in the L1 mental lexicon.

The results of Mara's study were later confirmed by other investigations. Laufer (1998) also believes that the connection between

L1 mental lexicons is semantic while the connection between the L2 mental lexicons is mainly phonological. Zhang's (2003) found that for a large proportion of words the L2 learners haven't built the meaningful connection between the L2 mental lexicon and the phonological connection holds the leading position.

However, Mara's interpretation of the results has also been criticized (Singleton, 1999; Namei, 2004). Mara (1983) claimed that the stimulus words in his test were "very common" L2 words. However, it was found that some of the stimulus words were quite rare items such as *claque*(herring-barrel), *toupee*(spinning-top), etc. These words were even uncommon to native speakers. And early studies show that native speakers are likely to produce phonological association when presented unfamiliar words. Similarly, L2 learners also tend to offer many clang responses when encountering the totally unfamiliar lexical items. Therefore, the subjects' responses to the rare lexical items in Mara's experiment cannot prove his finding that the structure of L2 mental lexicon is qualitatively different from that of L1 mental lexicon.

8.7.2 Semantic View

The semantic view holds that the structure of L2 mental lexicon is similar to that of L1 mental lexicon and semantic network plays a dominant role. Maréchal (1995) investigated the responses of two groups of students of French by using WA test. In the test, the stimulus words include 50 words chosen from Kent-Romanoff (1910) list and 50 French translations of those words. The results show that an overwhelming majority of responses in both L1 and L2 are based on meaning relations and only a tiny proportion are clang responses: 0.2% in L1 (English) and 3% in L2 (French).

This view was also confirmed by O'Gorman's (1996) study in which 22 Cantonese speakers with intermediate proficiency took a WA test. The result of the study is line with Maréchal's study. To be more precise, among the subjects' most common responses, the only clang associate was wealth (in response to health). In all other cases the responses have clear semantic links with the relevant stimuli.

Further evidence for the semantic view stemmed from Singleton's study. He conducted a longitudinal study under the auspices of the Trinity College Dublin Modern Languages Research Project (MLRP). Though this project did not focus specifically on the lexicon, the association tests conducted yielded the finding that among the advanced L2 learners the vast majority of responses were semantic-pragmatically related to the stimuli.

8.7.3 Syntactic View

According to the syntactic view, the words in the mind mainly have a syntagmatic relationship with each other. That is to say, links between words are mainly sequential or of collocation. Syntagmatic associates are words which frequently collocate with the stimulus item such as in sell-shirt, red-rose, steel-band, etc., (Singleton, 1999).

The syntagmatic view is advanced in a recent study by Wolter (2001). In an attempt to test the hypothesis that the L1 and the L2 mental lexicon are structurally similar, Wolter compared the response types of a group of 13 Japanese speakers of English as a second language and 9 native speakers of English, using two lists of stimulus words: One consists of higher frequency words and the other lower frequency ones. The percentages of different response types are: Native speakers produced 51.7% of paradigmatic responses, 41.0% of syntagmatic

responses, 7.6% of clang-other responses and 0% of no-responses. The L2 learners produced 19.7% of paradigmatic responses, 37.7% of syntagmatic responses, 35.1% of clang-other responses and 7.6% of no-responses.

Based on the findings, Wolter (2001) concluded that the L1 and the L2 mental lexicon, though sharing many similarities, are fundamentally different for words that are well known, with syntagmatic connections playing a more important role in organizing the words that comprise the non-native speaker mental lexicon.

8.8 Limitations of the Previous Researches

The WA test has made great contributions to the study of the mental lexicon, both in L1 and L2. The findings of WA studies are dependent, to a great extent, on the selection of stimulus words and the respondent. In previous WA studies, the stimulus words are mainly from the Kent-Romanoff (1910) list which was used as association "norms" in mental lexicon studies. However, researchers ignored the fact that the selection of stimulus words of the Kent-Romanoff (1910) list was based on a study by Sommer (1901) on mental health diagnoses using WA. Kent and Romanoff's list, like that of Sommer, was of course compiled not for linguistic purposes but in order to investigate methods for psychiatric screening (Fitzpatrick, 2007). In addition, it was compiled decades ago. Thus, they may not reflect well the dynamic nature of WA behavior. What's more, Kent-Romanoff's list includes many high-frequency words. It is widely believed that high-frequency cues will lead to more homogeneous and more predictable responses than lower-frequency words. For instance, the natural pairs (e.g., black, man and short) will always elicit the other half when responded to participants (e.g. , white, woman and tall). Obviously, the stereotyped responses can not exactly indicate the organization of L2 mental lexicon. Therefore, the first weakness lies in the selection of stimulus words. In the early empirical studies exploring Chinese English learners' L2 mental lexicon, researchers chose stimulus words from the traditional Kent-Romanoff's list.

The second weakness is that little consideration was given to the difference of participants' lexical knowledge between L1 and L2 studies. Without doubt, the vocabulary size of L2 learners is far smaller than that of native speakers. Thus, the common high-frequency words are presumably well-known to native speakers, but perhaps not so well-known to the L2 learners. If respondents are presented unfamiliar words, they will produce more clang responses. The data gathered in such researches cannot picture the structure of L2 mental lexicon well. Therefore, in the study of L2 associative behavior, frequency of stimulus words and respondents' lexical knowledge should be taken into consideration. The findings in the previous studies indicate that both native and non-native speakers produce anomalous and clang responses to low-frequency and unfamiliar words, which has no argument. Therefore, the researcher excluded low-frequency words and put emphasis on investigating the responses elicited by familiar words to Chinese students.

The third weakness of the previous WA tests lies in the classification of association responses. In most WA tests, researchers choose the conventional three-way classification of association responses to analyze response data. However the conventional classification of responses into paradigmatic, systematic and clang might not be precise enough to clearly describe Chinese learners' associative behavior.

8.9 Experimental Research

The present study was undertaken in an attempt to devise a WA test with an eye on addressing these two issues: selection of stimulus words and classification of responses. It was decided to make a significant break from past studies by opting not to use words from conventional sources such as the Kent-Romanoff or the Academic Word List. A relatively more precise categorization paradigm was employed, with an expectation to broaden the understanding of the organization of some Chinese L2 learners' mental lexicon.

8.9.1 Hypothesis

The present study aimed to investigate the nature of Chinese English learners' L2 mental lexicons by comparing the differences in the association responses between native speakers and Chinese learners. It was designed to probe the qualitative (classification of responses) and quantitative features (strength of primary responses, response commonality, response heterogeneity, response idiosyncrasy, and number of responses, etc.) of L2 learners' lexical knowledge

The present study is guided by the following hypotheses:

Hypothesis 1: There exist differences in associative strength between Chinese learners and native speakers.

Hypothesis 2: Chinese learners produce more form-based responses and less meaning-based and position-based responses than native speakers.

8.9.2 Participants

It is well known that the mental lexicon changes with age and language proficiency. Therefore, this study investigated the characteristics of the mental lexicon of subjects with similar proficiencies and ages.

Three classes of Chinese sophomores were randomly chosen as candidates, and given a picture naming test to select actual participants at the same level of English proficiency. Picture naming was used to assess English language proficiency and has demonstrated criterion validity (Lemmon & Gagging, 1989). The picture naming test participant selection procedure consisted of two steps: testing material selection and participant selection.

First, 68 pictures were randomly selected from 260 pictures used by Snodgrass and Vanderwart (1980). The selected pictures were presented on two sheets. A group of sophomores other than those candidates were each given two sheets of pictures with the following instructions: Please write down the name for each picture beside the picture as quickly as possible. The test was done during class time within a time limit of six minutes. The students' answers were scaled according to Snodgrass and Vanderwart (1980): If a picture was identified by its precise name (i.e., a picture of a horse labeled a "horse"), two points were awarded. If the picture was identified by a related name (i.e., a picture of a horse labeled a "donkey"), one point was awarded. If an unrelated name was used, or a response was completely missing, a score of zero was awarded (Lemmon & Gagging, 1989). The pictures on which more than 80 percent or less than 20 percent of the students got two points were excluded. Therefore, 56 pictures were chosen to be used in the next step.

Second, the same testing procedure as step one was done with the candidate participants with the 56 selected pictures. Those whose total score was 2 standard deviations higher or lower than the average score were not included. Then, 26, 40 and 38 participants were determined from the pre-selected three classes of candidate participants respectively (see Table 8-1).

Table 8-1 The participants' information

Number of participants		Age
Male	Female	
17	9	19±0. 84
37	1	19±0. 75
34	6	19±0. 67

All the participants took a multiple-choice vocabulary test and the result showed that the average size of their vocabulary size was 2,512 words. Therefore, the participants could be regarded as bilinguals of low L2 proficiency.

8. 9. 3 Materials

The selection of stimulus words is believed to be essential for developing a WA test. In order to avoid the problems of existing stimulus word lists, the researcher made an attempt to select stimulus words from the participants' textbooks (the second version of *New College English*, *Book One* and *Book Two*). In fact, for non-English majors, English textbook learning is usually their primary means of acquiring vocabulary, especially for low proficiency students. What's more, the mental lexicon of native and non-native speakers is in a constant state of change as new words are being learned and acquired. (Namei, 2004) Thus, it would be good if a WA test could reflect what the participants were learning at the time of the test.

In addition, two types of stimulus words would negatively influence the validity of WA tests. The first type is words which tend to elicit a very high proportion of primary responses, that is, words that have a strong "influence" on the response words such as *bread* (which in most cases produces the response *butter*) and *man* (*woman*). The second type is those that tend to have a low proportion of many responses (e.g., *trouble*), ultimately resulting in a large number of idiosyncratic responses. That would make it rather difficult for researchers to interpret the participants' responses.

Taking these facts into account, the researcher selected the stimulus words by using a spaced sampling procedure which is commonly used by L1 and L2 lexicon researchers. It involved selecting lexical items at a specific interval from a randomly determined starting point in the textbook. The sampling interval in this study took every first new boldface main entry from every 20th column, starting from the left-hand column on the first page of the glossary and resulting in a list of 85 words, which consist of 3 classes: nouns, verbs and adjectives.

The familiarity of the 85 words was evaluated by another 50 students of the same background as the participants at the same college on a 7-point Likert scale (with "1" meaning "not familiar," "7" "very familiar" and numbers between "1" and "7" standing for different degrees of familiarity). The average evaluation score was 6.43±0.25. Furthermore, the word frequency was looked up from the British National Corpus (a hundred million words) for each word and the average word frequency of the 85 stimulus words was 0.000128 ± 0.000104.

The stimulus words were divided into three groups (28, 29 and 28 words) at random, each of which would be used for one group of participants.

8.9.4 Classifications of Association Responses

The present study chose to adopt a new classification system which was proposed by Fitzpatrick (2006). This new classification system was based on response data from earlier work, the findings of previous studies, and a consideration of the literature on aspects of word knowledge (Nation, 2001). The association responses were classified into four broad categories:

• Meaning-based responses (i.e., those determined by semantic characteristics)

• Position-based responses (determined by syntactic and collocation characteristics)

• Form-based responses (determined by phonological, orthographical or morphological characteristics)

• Erratic responses (where no link between cue and responses was apparent, or no response at all was given)

The four categories were further divided into 10 subcategories, which made a more precise identification of response differences possible. Such evaluation criteria for the association type between a response and its stimulus word were predetermined according to Fitzpatrick's 2007 study, as shown in Table 8-2. That is, there was a total of 16 subcategories of possible types of associations between the participants' responses and the stimulus words.

Table 8-2 Four categories of associations, 16 subcategories of associations and the evaluation criteria for each association subcategory

Category	Subcategory	Criteria	Example
Form-based association	Derivation	The response word is a derivation of the stimulus word (DR).	*health→healthy*[*]
	Change of part of speech	The response and the stimulus word are of the same meaning but different parts of speech (CPS).	*choice→choose*
	Compounds	The response is a correct compound word of the stimulus word (Cmp).	*life→lifetime*
Form-based association	Addition or omission of a letter	The response is a correct word that is formed by adding one letter to or deleting one letter from the stimulus word (AOL).	*thin→thing*
	Similar in form but not similar in meaning	The response looks or sounds similar to but does not mean the same as the stimulus word (FnotM).	*worry→marry*
	Repetition	The response is the repetition of the cue word (RP).	*accept→accept*
Meaning-based association	Synonym	The response is a synonym of the stimulus word (Sn).	*accept→receive*
	Personal feeling	The response clearly indicates the participants' feeling towards the concept the stimulus words represent (PF).	*noise→boring*
	Context related	The response has some kind of semantic relation to the stimulus word (CR).	*desert→hot*
Position-based association	Consecutive xy collocation	The response usually follows the stimulus word to make a usually fixed expression (CxyC).	*red→rose* *accept→for*
	Consecutive yx collocation	The response usually precedes the stimulus word to make a usually fixed expression (CyxC).	*life→love* *for→look*

续表

Category	Subcategory	Criteria	Example
Erratic association	Wrong derivation	The response is a wrong derivation of the stimulus word (WDR).	*poor→poory*
	Illegal creation	The response looks like an English word but is created by making some changes to the stimulus word spelling (IllC).	*bee→beel*
	Spelling error	The response is a wrongly spelt word but seems to reflect a semantic relation to the stimulus word (SE).	*fail→ture*
Erratic association	No relation	The response is a correct word but has no relation to the stimulus word (NR).	*discuss→four*
	Letter cluster	The response is just a cluster of letters (LC).	*review→wsk*

* cue word→response, e.g., *health→healthy*

8.9.5 Procedures

The test was conducted during normal class hours, and each group was tested with a sheet of cue words. The three groups took the test in different classrooms at almost the same time. Before the test, the following instructions were read to the subjects and then explained in Chinese: "Please write down the first word you think of when you read each of the words listed. There are no right or wrong answers, so try not to take a long time considering your response." During the test, the participants were not allowed to consult any dictionaries or reference books, nor were they allowed to discuss with each other. The test lasted for about five minutes for each group of participants.

The association responses generated by the participants were keyed in Microsoft Access databases. If the responses were illegible or blank, they were regarded as invalid. The researcher found that the valid response percentage was 99.1%.

Then the association between each response and its stimulus word was classified independently by two raters who were English teachers, according to the predetermined association evaluation criteria. The inter-rater agreement ratio between the two teachers was 89%. For each case where the two raters had different evaluations, another rater was invited to make the final classification.

Native speakers' responses to the cue words came from a large, freely available database of English association norms, the Edinburgh Associative Thesaurus (EAT) (http://www.eat.rl.ac.uk/). The association types were evaluated in the same way for the native speakers' responses as for those of the participants.

8.9.6 Results

For the participants, the association strength of each stimulus word was calculated by dividing the frequency of each response by the total number of valid responses. The greatest strength is called the primary association strength. For native speakers, the different response words and the primary association strength of each stimulus word was looked up from EAT. Similarly, the four category association strengths of each stimulus word were calculated for both the participants and native speakers by dividing the frequencies of the four categories of associations by the total number of valid responses. Then statistical analyses were done with SPSS 16.0 on the number of responses, the primary association strength and the category association strengths to make a comparison between WA performance of the participants and native speakers.

(1) A paired-samples t test of the primary association strength for

the participants and that of native speakers indicates that the former (0. 24±0. 14) is significantly lower than the latter (0. 28±0. 08), $t_{(85)}=3.527$, $p<0.005$ (see Table 8-3). This indicates that the participants might have a relatively poorer concentricity of association than native speakers for the same stimulus words. According to spreading-activation theory, if one node is more closely related to some nodes than to other nodes in the network of memory, the connection lines between the closely related nodes could be thicker than those between the less closely related nodes. The finding that the participants' primary association strength was relatively weaker than that of native speakers probably means that the activation of one English word in the English mental lexicon of the Chinese learners might spread to more other words but with a lower strength than that of native speakers.

Table 8-3 A paired-samples *t* test to the primary association strength for the participants and that of native speakers

		$M \pm SD$
The participants	Primary association strength	0. 241±0. 143
	Average association strength	0. 024±0. 006
Native speakers	Primary association strength	0. 281±0. 082
	Average association strength	0. 055±0. 014

(2) Table 8-4 shows that the primary association strength of the participants was not correlated with that of native speakers, $r=0.078$, $p>0.10$. The correlations between primary association strength and average association strength were $r=0.689$, $p<0.01$, for native speakers and were $r=0.227$, $p<0.05$ for the participants. This means that for some stimulus words, the participants had high association

concentricity, while the association concentricity of native speakers was low. For some other stimulus words, however, native speakers had high association concentricity, while the association concentricity of the participants was low.

Table 8-4 Primary association strength (PAS) and average association strength (AAS) of native speakers (NS) and the participants (P)

		PAS of NS	AAS of NS	PAS of p	AAS of P
PAS of NS	Pearson Correlation	1	.689**	.078	.207
	Sig. (2-tailed)		.000	.475	.056
	N	86	86	86	86
AAS of NS	Pearson Correlation	.689**	1	.030	.341**
	Sig. (2-tailed)	.000		.781	.001
	N	86	86	86	86
PAS of p	Pearson Correlation	.078	.030	1	.227*
	Sig. (2-tailed)	.475	.781		.035
	N	86	86	86	86
AAS of P	Pearson Correlation	.207	.341**	.227*	1
	Sig. (2-tailed)	.056	.001	.035	
	N	86	86	86	86

** Correlation is significant at the 0.01 level (2-tailed).

* Correlation is significant at the 0.05 level (2-tailed).

(3) Because each stimulus word corresponded to one primary strength and four category association strengths for both the participants and native speakers, the association between the non-repeated response word and its stimulus word must be one of the four association categories. It seems that the primary strength of non-repeated response words to all the stimulus words covers different association categories for the participants and for native speakers (see Table 8-5). As the table shows, the primary strength of non-repeated response words for native speakers corresponded to only two association categories, covering four subcategories, but for the participants it covered sixteen subcategories

from all four association categories. Furthermore, the participants seemed to have a stronger tendency for form-based associations than for position-or meaning-based associations.

Table 8-5 The count and percentage of the frequencies of non-repeated response words that correspond to different association sub-categories and association categories for both the participants and native speakers

	AC	Sub AC	Count	Percentage
Native speakers	Position-based	CxyC	22	25.9
		CyxC	1	1.2
	Meaning-based	Sn	40	47.1
		PF	23	27.1
The participants	Position-based	CxyC	15	17.7
	Meaning-based	Sn	15	17.7
		PF	11	12.8
	Form-based	FnotM	20	23.3
		CPS	4	4.7
		DR	17	20.0
		AOL	2	2.4
	Erratic	SE	1	1.2

A 2 (the participants versus native speakers) * 4 (position-based, meaning-based, form-based and erratic association categories) two-factor repeated measurement variance analysis was conducted. The results (see Table 8-6) show that the main effect of the change from the participants to native speakers was significant, $F(1,84)=6.508$, $p<0.05$, $\eta^2=0.07$, and the main effect of association categories was significant, $F(3,252)=8.311$, $p<0.01$, $\eta^2=0.089$. The interaction between association categories and the change from the participants to native speakers was not significant. It is obvious that the participants had different category association strengths from those of native speakers for different association categories; however, paired-samples t tests were conducted to make a comparison between each of the participants' and native speakers' category association strengths. For position-based ($t_{(85)} = 7.461$, $p < 0.001$) and meaning-based ($t_{(85)} = 17.663$, $p < 0.001$) associations, native speakers had stronger association strengths than the participants. For form-based ($t_{(85)} = -27.271$, $p < 0.001$) and erratic ($t_{(85)} = -11.226$, $p < 0.001$) associations, however, native speakers had weaker association strengths than the participants. Therefore, the participants tended to have form-based rather than meaning-based association in the WA test. This is consistent with Namei 2004 in that low-L2-proficiency bilinguals may make form-based rather than meaning-based associations during WA tasks.

Table 8-6 The average category association strengths for the participants and native speakers

	Association categories	$M \pm SD$
Native speakers	Position-based	0.283±0.191
	Form-based	0.033±0.035
	Meaning-based	0.635±0.196
	Erratic	0.033±0.035
The participants	Position-based	0.137±0.112
	Form-based	0.448±0.144
	Meaning-based	0.272±0.155
	Erratic	0.134±0.076

(4) Bivariate correlations were done between the four category association strengths and the stimulus word familiarity evaluation scores for the participants and between the four category association strengths and the stimulus word frequency for native speakers. The results reveals

that the stimulus word familiarity evaluation scores were negatively correlated with the erratic association strength ($r = -0.463$, $p < 0.001$) but not correlated with other category association strengths for the participants. It is understandable that the more familiar the participants were with stimulus words, the less possible it was for them to make erratic associations. However, the fact that no correlation was found between the participants' other category association strengths and the stimulus word familiarity evaluation calls for specific explanation. It might be possible that the participants know different aspects of stimulus words to different levels. For example, they could clearly remember the meanings of a word but not know its usage well. They could clearly know how to use another word but not be confident about this word's meanings. Therefore, the stimulus word could seem familiar to the participants not because they knew each aspect of the word and its usage well but rather because they only knew some specific aspects well. This explanation seems reasonable when we take the participants' English learning style into consideration. For example, most Chinese college students try to enrich their English vocabulary not by using the language as much as possible but by of memorizing single word entries from a glossary book. This finding seems to confirm the validity of the data analysis process of the present study.

8.9.7 Discussion

Based on the above results, the characteristics of the L2 mental lexicon of Chinese English learners can be summarized as follows:

First, the participants did show some evidence of L2 semantic organization, which might be mainly dependent on translation. That is, they first translated the cue words into Chinese in order to understand their semantic properties and then produced the responses based on translation equivalents. This could be illustrated by the data on position-based association. For example, to the stimulus word *view*, the participants responded with *book*, and *TV*. However, among the 43 responses produced by native speakers, there were no responses like *book*, *TV* or *television*. This example reveals some particular associative process for the participants. They must have translated the stimulus word *view* into a Chinese word 看 according to their memory and then activated Chinese phrases such as 看书 or 看电视 based on Chinese semantic knowledge. The third step was to translate these Chinese phrases back into corresponding English expressions such as *view book*, *view TV* or *view television*. In the end, they wrote down the responses *book*, *TV* or *television*.

According to Jiang's three stages of lexical development in L2, the participants' lexicons could be at the second stage. That is, their L2 lexical items at this stage might be considered lexical items without lemmas; in other words, the lemma structure is empty. Little semantic, syntactic and morphological information is created and established within the lexical entry in such a process. Therefore, the use of L2 words depends on the activation of the links between L2 words and their L1 translations. As one's experience in L2 increases, stronger associations are developed between L2 words and their L1 equivalents, i.e., the simultaneous activation of L2 words' forms and the lemma information of L1 equivalents. So information in L1 lemma may be copied or attached to L2 lexical forms to form lexical entries that have L2 lexical forms but semantic and syntactic information of their L1 equivalents. And since morphological information is usually language-specific, and thus less susceptible to transfer, no morphological specifications are contained in

the lexical entry at this stage. The full development of lexical competence has a final stage when the semantic, syntactic, and morphological specifications of an L2 word are integrated into the lexical entry. At this stage, a lexical entry in L2 will be very similar to a lexical entry in L1 in terms of both representation and proceedings.

Second, the participants could produce some position-based responses based on their L2 semantic network. From Table 3, we can find that the participants provided a large number of consecutive responses, particularly responses on consecutive collocations. For example, the stimulus words *communicate*, *pay* and *worry* elicited the responses *with*, *for* and *about* respectively. In addition, based on word clusters, the stimulus words *table*, *fresh*, *bad* and *life* elicited the responses *tennis*, *man*, *news* and *experience* respectively. In fact, as the Table 4 shows, both the participants and native speakers like to make consecutive associations, which are position-based associations. This result is in line with the finding in Fitzpatrick (2007) that the most popular response type of native speakers' responses is the consecutive collocation. Although compared with native speakers, the participants had fewer collocations available, this result indicates that they were aware of chunks and tended to store language in chunks.

Third, the majority of the participants' responses were classified as form-based associations (43 out of 85). They seemed to be so dependent on word forms that they created some new words which do not even exist. For example, *weariness*was elicited by *wear* and *poory* by *poor*. What's more, spelling errors became one of the primary responses, which had negative correlation with word familiarity. All the above pieces of evidence indicate that the organization of the participants' mental lexicon was to a great degree constructed according to word forms rather than meanings. One possible reason for this phenomenon might be as follows. In classroom teaching, English teachers place too much emphasis on word formation teaching. Students are exposed to a variety of word-formation exercises and tests. Although in second language acquisition word formation is one of the major mechanisms for the expansion of the vocabulary, it may make the learners produce a lot of wrong "words" if they do not have a good mastery of word formation rules.

Fourth, the participants' responses show a less degree of commonalty compared with native speakers'. Native speakers tend to cluster their associations around a small number of commonly given responses. For example, a cursory look at EAT shows that 81% of native speakers' responses to the stimulus word *blanket* cluster around only 10 associations (*bed*, *warm*, *sheet*, *electric*, *cover*, *warmth*, *wool*, *soft*, *bath*, *snow*) and only 19% of all responses are idiosyncratic in nature (Namei, 2004). In this study, native speakers' responses only cover four association sub-categories belonging to two association categories. This also shows the high degree of commonality of their responses. This high degree of associative commonality has been interpreted as indicative of native likeness of associative behavior by some researchers who started comparing the degree of L2 learners' associative commonality to that of native speakers. In addition, lower associative commonality was often indicative of unstable meaning connections. Therefore, it is safe to draw the conclusion that the participants might have not established stable semantic networks.

Generally, the differences in terms of associative patterns, associative strength and numbers of responses show that the structure of the participants' mental lexicon was significantly different from that of

native speakers'. It appears to lack systematic and stable connections, and this confirms previous findings (Mara, 1978). The lack of tight semantic connections between words in the L2 mental lexicon compared with the L1 mental lexicon is supported by research applying the graph theoretical principles to empirical WA data in order to investigate the relative densities of the L1 and L2 networks. This body of research includes Welsh (1988) and Meara (1992). They found that the L2 mental lexicon was less dense than the L1 mental lexicon. That is to say, there were far fewer semantic connections between words in the L2 mental lexicon than those in the L1 mental lexicon.

According to the extended network model, orthographically linked connection of words in the main L2 mental lexicon show that L2 lexicons are stored at a lexeme level which is far away from the appropriate conceptual level. Words at the lexeme level are certainly not mastered. In comparison with the L1 mental lexicon, the semantic network in the mental lexicon is underdeveloped. When semantics play a predominant role in the organization of the L2 mental lexicon, the semantic relationship is fully established and the L2 lexicon network resembles that of the L1 mental lexicon.

8.10 Implications for L2 Vocabulary Teaching

From the above analysis, we can conclude that L2 learners have not established well-organized semantic networks and the connection between words is mainly based on forms. These findings may give a clue to L2 vocabulary acquisition.

(1) It has been proven that words stored in semantic networks can be retrieved quickly and long-lasting. The presence of semantically

related words is conductive to the lexical access. Namely, semantically related words are more quickly recognized than words sharing no sense relations. Thus, semantic network is an ideal structure of mental lexicon.

The words in the same semantic field tend to be stored together. For example words may be classified into musical instrument and vehicle (manufactured); vegetable and insect (naturally occurring) and so on. They should be learnt together not only because of their closeness in meaning but also because of their frequent co-occurrence in the same context. The learning of one will help to learn the meaning of the other.

In native speakers' mental lexicon, semantic networks play a predominant role. However L2 learners' semantic network is underdeveloped. Particularly less proficient L2 learners lack stable semantic networks. And words in their networks are loosely connected. To help L2 learners construct semantic networks, teachers need adopt some effective strategies in vocabulary teaching. They may organize some meaningful exercise or classroom activities which promote formation of association and build up students' semantic network. For example, semantic elaboration is a good choice. Semantic elaboration includes two important techniques: semantic feature analysis and semantic mapping. Semantic feature analysis is to analyze components of words. In semantic feature analysis students are asked to distinguish meaning features. Semantic mapping generally refers to brainstorming associations which is a bit like free word association. For example, when given a word 'faithfulness', students are asked to write down what they thought of. Some L2 learners generated the following words or phrases: cat, friend, family, reliance, trust, believe in friendship, dishonest, unfaithful, marriage, and love. After clustering words which they felt

went together, they mapped the relationships between these words. Over time, the learners may add new words to the maps. These semantic exercises stimulate students to explore the relationships between the new word and words already known and finally they will expand learners' vocabulary by integrating new words with old and promote deep levels of encoding.

Words learnt in their conceptual structures are better understood than words learnt in isolation, for conceptual structures provide answers to such questions as whether there is any default agent or object for an action word and what is the usual instrument. These questions are crucial to the appropriate use of an action word. Words that are relevant to the same topic should be learnt together, because they are related in meaning and because they often co-occur in a certain context. If these words are stored in the mental lexicon together, the activation of one would help activate the others, which would be most convenient for language production.

(2) L2 learners can depend on their knowledge of word parts to acquire new vocabulary. The present study shows that Chinese English learners' responses are, to a large degree, dependent on formed-based association. And the students produced many non-existent words according to word formation knowledge. The results of the word class section suggest that students did not have a very good mastery of the derivational forms of a word. There may be some reasons accounting for this result. One of them is that teachers put great emphasis on word formation teaching but the students did not grasp the word formation rules, in other words, they can not use the rules well but memorize the derivation by rote. Their morphological knowledge such as the prefix, suffix, and roots of words are sometimes stored separately. There is no

doubt that if students can grasp some basic word formation, they will enlarge their vocabulary rapidly. Therefore, to help students better learn and use word formation, teachers need systematically teach the important affixes and word roots in target language. A good approach to learning word formation is to give students word parts and then ask them to add prefix or suffix. In this way, students can learn knowledge of word unit well.

(3) Words in context are recognized more quickly than isolated words. The proper context can quicken the recognition of words and eliminate the ambiguity of words. When a preceding context primes a word, the lexical access happens and the dominant meaning of the word is selected. In the lexical access experiment of Swinney (1979), the subjects were asked to listen to the following sentence: Rumor had it that, for years, the government building had been plagues with problems. The man was not surprised when he found several spiders, roaches, and other bugs in the corner of his room. With the guide of context, the subject easily recognized the meaning of bug as a kind of insect, but not a kind of tapping device. Thus, vocabulary should be taught in context. With the appropriate context as clues, words can leave a deeper trace in the learner's memory and have more chances to be activated. Teachers can ask students to read a passage and then ask them to guess the meaning of difficult words in the passage, which a good way of teaching words in context.

(4) It is very clear now that reliance on L1 is an inevitable stage in the forming and development of L2 lexical representations and a key factor influencing the development of L2 lexical competence. Therefore, it is of great necessity for learners to consciously increase the input of L2 lemma information and cut down their reliance on L1 lemma, so as to

ensure the balanced development of the semantic, syntactic, morphological and formal information within L2 lexical entry. Only when the diverse information is highly integrated into the lexical entry and has become an indispensable part of it can connections between L2 words and concepts be strengthened and lexical competence further develop so as to ensure fast activation and accurate retrieval.

(5) Learning L2 words with the help of their L1 translations is indeed a rather convenient and effective method in the early stages. However. it may mislead the learners into thinking that words in two languages have a one-for-one semantic relationship. In fact, many words in one language do not have a true equivalent in another language. So not all L2 words have corresponding L1 translations and not all L1 translations have the same degree of semantic overlap with L2 words. Therefore, in college L2 vocabulary teaching, teachers should try to use target language instead of translation of L2. And the students should be encouraged to use L2 monolingual dictionaries.

(6) According to word frequency effect, frequent words are recognized more quickly than infrequent words. Commonly-used words and meanings appear to be in a state of greater readiness than less-often-used words and meanings. Thus, teachers should increase input of frequent words and learners must be given sufficient exposure to the vocabulary. For L2 English learners, one efficient way to ensure multiple exposure is reading extensively. Therefore, extensive reading should be encouraged.

(7) Collocation relationships appear to have powerful and lasting links in the lexicon (Aitchison, 1987). Providing opportunities to practice collocations is a worthwhile activity. Learning commonly used collocations as chunks, groups of words which frequently occur

together, is very efficient and more accurate than learning individual words. Learners should learn to store new words in lexical chunks rather than individually, which is a good way of enlarging vocabulary. In addition, it will ensure conciseness and precision of expression in productive language.

(8) Orthographical representation of words must be reinforced again and again. The present research shows that to some prompt words, the students' primary strength is erratic association, which shows that they have not grasped orthographical representation of words. Through reinforcement, lexical knowledge can be kept in the learner's permanent memory and retrieved at any time.

(9) To make sure that L2 learners have built an appropriate lexemic representation of the newly acquired L2 lexis, the teacher has to devise a number of exercises focusing on phonetic, orthographic, and morphological properties of new words.

(10) WAs can also be applied to direct vocabulary teaching. Association based on vocabulary instruction allows lexical items to be examined as a part of the larger lexical network, rather than just individual items. It stimulates students to examine the relationship between the novel items and words already known. Therefore, it seems important that classroom instruction includes activities that help students not only acquire the meaning of new words, but also enrich their knowledge of previously met words, resulting in richer and more accessible lexical network, and consequently, more efficient vocabulary usage.

8.11 Conclusion

The general aim of the present study was to explore the nature of the L2 mental lexicon of Chinese English learners. Overall, the quantitative and the qualitative features of the mental lexicon of Chinese learners are different from those of native speakers. The differences exist in the strength of the primary response, response commonality, response heterogeneity, availability of responses, number of responses, and classification of responses. To be precise, their association is too much dependent on forms, and the responses of Chinese learners tend to scatter compared with those of native speakers. The connections between words in the L2 mental lexicon lack tight semantic links. The results of the experiments offer some insights for L2 vocabulary acquisition.

Although the present study has revealed, to a certain extent, the organization patterns of the L2 mental lexicon of Chinese learners, it still has some limitations.

In this study, one of the criteria for choosing SWs is the frequency. The SWs in the study are all high-frequency words in English. The reason for leaving out low-frequency words is that they may not elicit the responses needed to reveal the organization of the L2 mental lexicon. However, the investigation of individual words of both high and low frequency is suggested for future researches. It will become more convincing to make generalization about the structure of the L2 mental lexicon.

The subjects in this research are at the similar proficiency of L2 language. In fact, researchers have assumed that as learners gain in proficiency the structure of their mental lexicon comes to resemble that of native speakers and WA tests are a quick and easy means of proficiency assessment. Recently, a significant number of studies have experimented with the structure of the L2 lexicon at different levels of L2 proficiency (Randall, 1980; Kruse, Pinehurst & Sherwood, Smith, 1987). One of the earliest studies of the effect of language proficiency on associative behavior was conducted by Lambert (1956). Lambert compared the continuous WA tests to American students of French at undergraduate and graduate level in comparison with native speakers of French. His findings suggested that the number of responses increases with an increase in the level of language proficiency. Native speakers gave more responses than graduate students, who in turn gave more responses than undergraduate students.

Sideman (1993) studied the associative responses of native speakers of different ages and found that the systematic-paradigmatic shift in response type occurred too, which implies that response types reflect level of proficiency in a particular language whether it is L1 and L2. Further evidence in support of this view is provided by her another experiment research in which four groups of English learners of different levels of proficiency took WA tests. By comparing the responses of these four groups she found that the proportion of clang and systematic associations was found to decrease as the learners became more proficient.

Piper and Leicester (1980) used WA tests to compare the vocabulary of native speakers with advanced and intermediate Japanese learners of English. Their findings showed that vocabulary of L2 learners follows the developmental patterns of L1. Overall, the studies showed that there is subtle relationship between associative patterns and language proficiency.

Appendix

The numbers of different response words, primary association strengths and category association strengths for the participants and native speakers for the same SWs*.

SWs	NoR		PAS		CAS							
					P		F		M		E	
	Ps	NS	Ps	NS	Ps	NS	Ps	NS	Ps	NS	Ps	NS
sleep	45	15	0.16	0.21	0.16	0.06	0.01	0.59	0.83	0.26	0.00	0.09
feel	50	21	0.21	0.15	0.40	0.32	0.04	0.47	0.53	0.15	0.01	0.06
die	49	14	0.16	0.24	0.07	0.06	0.15	0.65	0.74	0.26	0.01	0.03
happy	43	36	0.35	0.07	0.14	0.06	0.02	0.37	0.81	0.39	0.01	0.19
noise	48	17	0.15	0.12	0.18	0.03	0.01	0.47	0.74	0.50	0.04	0.00
believe	51	19	0.16	0.11	0.41	0.18	0.05	0.54	0.51	0.18	0.02	0.11
other	37	12	0.12	0.14	0.70	0.14	0.07	0.68	0.16	0.14	0.06	0.04
sad	41	16	0.30	0.29	0.11	0.00	0.05	0.50	0.76	0.43	0.03	0.07
health	54	32	0.10	0.50	0.22	0.14	0.00	0.67	0.75	0.11	0.00	0.06
life	42	36	0.44	0.06	0.16	0.30	0.04	0.51	0.78	0.13	0.01	0.06
care	54	14	0.11	0.24	0.35	0.29	0.14	0.62	0.48	0.09	0.00	0.00
change	53	22	0.20	0.18	0.60	0.29	0.02	0.47	0.36	0.12	0.00	0.12

续表

SWs	CAS											
	NoR		PAS		P		F		M		E	
	Ps	NS	Ps	NS	Ps	NS	Ps	NS	Ps	NS	Ps	NS
empty	39	14	0.47	0.59	0.26	0.12	0.01	0.15	0.71	0.65	0.01	0.09
sound	44	23	0.32	0.12	0.24	0.15	0.00	0.41	0.75	0.35	0.00	0.09
table	30	26	0.36	0.19	0.35	0.11	0.00	0.27	0.61	0.46	0.03	0.16
drink	48	18	0.20	0.11	0.42	0.29	0.05	0.39	0.51	0.25	0.00	0.07
meat	53	17	0.12	0.21	0.14	0.07	0.00	0.57	0.83	0.21	0.02	0.14
sun	38	17	0.25	0.14	0.32	0.07	0.01	0.43	0.64	0.46	0.03	0.04
possible	39	18	0.38	0.24	0.17	0.06	0.02	0.56	0.71	0.21	0.09	0.18
safe	45	16	0.19	0.24	0.35	0.03	0.03	0.50	0.50	0.47	0.11	0.00
choice	58	17	0.08	0.08	0.37	0.11	0.08	0.68	0.48	0.03	0.02	0.19
hungry	43	21	0.24	0.14	0.06	0.00	0.03	0.41	0.88	0.54	0.01	0.05
move	52	23	0.09	0.19	0.52	0.05	0.05	0.59	0.41	0.22	0.01	0.14
see	39	18	0.15	0.24	0.10	0.05	0.11	0.43	0.64	0.43	0.14	0.08
worry	65	17	0.09	0.19	0.35	0.24	0.06	0.51	0.56	0.08	0.02	0.16
address	38	18	0.38	0.25	0.09	0.11	0.02	0.50	0.80	0.29	0.07	0.11
season	27	15	0.16	0.18	0.17	0.00	0.01	0.29	0.82	0.46	0.00	0.25
weather	38	15	0.24	0.21	0.19	0.21	0.02	0.50	0.76	0.18	0.02	0.11
dark	32	23	0.41	0.22	0.12	0.08	0.02	0.38	0.84	0.41	0.01	0.14
sea	55	19	0.08	0.14	0.42	0.18	0.01	0.39	0.51	0.36	0.06	0.07
discuss	36	24	0.43	0.22	0.05	0.16	0.01	0.41	0.90	0.22	0.01	0.19
strong	33	25	0.48	0.22	0.13	0.27	0.01	0.32	0.80	0.08	0.06	0.27
discover	50	15	0.40	0.21	0.09	0.07	0.02	0.57	0.86	0.25	0.03	0.11
office	44	19	0.15	0.14	0.23	0.25	0.02	0.25	0.67	0.36	0.08	0.14
difficult	33	14	0.34	0.21	0.15	0.09	0.01	0.35	0.82	0.44	0.02	0.12
interest	60	16	0.12	0.09	0.15	0.09	0.03	0.59	0.80	0.24	0.01	0.09

续表

SWs	CAS											
	NoR		PAS		P		F		M		E	
	Ps	NS	Ps	NS	Ps	NS	Ps	NS	Ps	NS	Ps	NS
laugh	41	20	0. 28	0. 22	0. 09	0. 22	0. 01	0. 14	0. 85	0. 51	0. 03	0. 14
poor	42	32	0. 38	0. 07	0. 22	0. 07	0. 06	0. 28	0. 64	0. 49	0. 08	0. 13
develop	55	20	0. 12	0. 24	0. 30	0. 15	0. 03	0. 56	0. 61	0. 06	0. 03	0. 24
dear	40	18	0. 12	0. 21	0. 22	0. 21	0. 02	0. 50	0. 66	0. 18	0. 07	0. 11
outside	25	11	0. 54	0. 07	0. 12	0. 14	0. 01	0. 18	0. 84	0. 61	0. 02	0. 07
fail	37	18	0. 24	0. 14	0. 18	0. 05	0. 14	0. 46	0. 67	0. 35	0. 00	0. 14
society	63	19	0. 18	0. 21	0. 09	0. 24	0. 03	0. 26	0. 84	0. 29	0. 03	0. 21
wear	30	36	0. 33	0. 08	0. 81	0. 43	0. 05	0. 31	0. 10	0. 06	0. 03	0. 17
full	37	16	0. 51	0. 21	0. 19	0. 07	0. 02	0. 57	0. 78	0. 25	0. 00	0. 11
act	42	18	0. 27	0. 16	0. 36	0. 05	0. 07	0. 76	0. 52	0. 08	0. 02	0. 11
succeed	46	16	0. 18	0. 22	0. 03	0. 03	0. 17	0. 41	0. 75	0. 38	0. 04	0. 19
chair	36	16	0. 16	0. 21	0. 16	0. 00	0. 06	0. 21	0. 77	0. 54	0. 01	0. 21
weigh	37	12	0. 15	0. 19	0. 34	0. 00	0. 05	0. 49	0. 56	0. 41	0. 03	0. 11
accept	37	20	0. 13	0. 19	0. 32	0. 16	0. 01	0. 35	0. 60	0. 32	0. 05	0. 11
fool	47	19	0. 18	0. 14	0. 11	0. 00	0. 01	0. 61	0. 80	0. 21	0. 06	0. 18
test	46	21	0. 16	0. 14	0. 46	0. 21	0. 03	0. 50	0. 44	0. 07	0. 07	0. 21
limit	36	25	0. 25	0. 18	0. 33	0. 15	0. 03	0. 50	0. 61	0. 12	0. 01	0. 18
humor	31	24	0. 24	0. 16	0. 07	0. 03	0. 02	0. 46	0. 88	0. 22	0. 00	0. 24
wood	53	19	0. 19	0. 14	0. 21	0. 04	0. 00	0. 43	0. 71	0. 32	0. 07	0. 21
pain	53	54	0. 17	0. 06	0. 16	0. 07	0. 02	0. 49	0. 80	0. 30	0. 00	0. 12
skill	52	30	0. 10	0. 08	0. 16	0. 07	0. 06	0. 56	0. 69	0. 15	0. 05	0. 20
communicate	44	16	0. 27	0. 21	0. 14	0. 24	0. 00	0. 32	0. 83	0. 29	0. 02	0. 15
relax	52	25	0. 18	0. 09	0. 05	0. 09	0. 01	0. 56	0. 88	0. 18	0. 03	0. 18
sex	47	19	0. 09	0. 15	0. 03	0. 03	0. 01	0. 29	0. 87	0. 59	0. 08	0. 03

续表

SWs	CAS											
	NoR		PAS		P		F		M		E	
	Ps	NS	Ps	NS	Ps	NS	Ps	NS	Ps	NS	Ps	NS
flood	33	16	0.46	0.14	0.02	0.07	0.01	0.61	0.97	0.21	0.00	0.11
low	28	15	0.67	0.25	0.14	0.18	0.01	0.36	0.85	0.39	0.00	0.07
main	53	15	0.16	0.18	0.61	0.07	0.01	0.57	0.35	0.07	0.02	0.25
prepare	51	25	0.13	0.15	0.45	0.24	0.02	0.47	0.40	0.15	0.11	0.12
produce	56	18	0.12	0.24	0.40	0.09	0.07	0.53	0.47	0.15	0.05	0.24
thin	33	22	0.34	0.22	0.15	0.16	0.01	0.27	0.77	0.43	0.06	0.14
view	43	19	0.10	0.14	0.32	0.11	0.02	0.25	0.57	0.43	0.06	0.21
pear	23	16	0.29	0.11	0.12	0.00	0.02	0.82	0.83	0.11	0.01	0.07
service	56	21	0.12	0.15	0.75	0.03	0.00	0.21	0.22	0.38	0.00	0.35
fresh	44	17	0.09	0.32	0.58	0.14	0.04	0.54	0.37	0.14	0.00	0.14
bill	46	18	0.22	0.18	0.14	0.04	0.02	0.54	0.63	0.36	0.18	0.07
press	49	27	0.09	0.09	0.51	0.12	0.01	0.41	0.37	0.15	0.11	0.29
silence	36	22	0.20	0.26	0.26	0.06	0.00	0.38	0.71	0.32	0.02	0.21
agree	42	12	0.20	0.26	0.40	0.26	0.02	0.59	0.56	0.06	0.01	0.09
bad	33	14	0.56	0.14	0.19	0.10	0.04	0.38	0.75	0.38	0.02	0.10
catch	46	21	0.17	0.18	0.58	0.26	0.03	0.44	0.31	0.15	0.07	0.12
knock	40	15	0.31	0.24	0.20	0.59	0.07	0.18	0.71	0.18	0.00	0.06
later	32	16	0.17	0.28	0.45	0.14	0.02	0.34	0.51	0.34	0.00	0.14
lose	43	14	0.24	0.11	0.27	0.11	0.11	0.61	0.58	0.21	0.02	0.07
pay	43	24	0.29	0.23	0.52	0.33	0.06	0.33	0.35	0.08	0.05	0.21
raise	41	21	0.18	0.18	0.39	0.08	0.01	0.47	0.50	0.37	0.08	0.08
review	60	29	0.09	0.14	0.48	0.08	0.04	0.38	0.39	0.14	0.03	0.41
thank	18	11	0.74	0.21	0.81	0.39	0.00	0.57	0.17	0.00	0.02	0.04
tooth	32	18	0.19	0.11	0.66	0.03	0.02	0.54	0.29	0.27	0.00	0.16

续表

SWs	CAS											
	NoR		PAS		P		F		M		E	
	Ps	NS	Ps	NS	Ps	NS	Ps	NS	Ps	NS	Ps	NS
wild	57	18	0. 08	0. 14	0. 51	0. 35	0. 01	0. 46	0. 45	0. 05	0. 00	0. 14

*：NoR，PAS，CAS，P，F，M，E，Ps and NS mean the number of responses，the primary association strength and the category association strengths，position－based association，form－based association，meaning－based association，erratic association，participants，and native speakers respectively

Chapter Nine Lexis Acquisition in Multimedia Environment

9.1 Introduction to the Application of Vocabulary Motivation

For most students in learning language, the difficulty they first meet is usually the memory of words.

Vocabulary is an important part of a language as well as the basis of linguistic abilities. The vocabulary quantity is an important standard to evaluate a learner's English level. Without adequate vocabulary knowledge, a second language learner's conversational fluency and reading comprehension will meet difficulties. Vocabulary is the foundation of a language. Students' competence of language is closely related to their vocabulary capacity which could influence their acquisition of listening, reading, writing and translation. It is the most important factor in academic achievement for students' language acquisition.

In the language learning and teaching, vocabulary has always been a neglect and weak point. Wilkins (1972) said "Linguists have had

remarkably little to say about the vocabulary and one can find few studies which could be of any practical interests for language teachers". A decade later, Meara (1982) mentioned that vocabulary had received short shift from applied linguistics. Ellis (1995) expressed the view that the situation had not changed significantly. This situation may be due to the fact that many teachers assume that vocabulary instruction amounts to telling students to guess the meaning of a word with regard to the grammatical and pragmatic context in which the word is found. But unfortunately students sometimes do not use context clues properly because of their poor vocabulary knowledge, low vocabulary capacity. Moreover, Parry's (1993) study found that a single context hardly gives enough information for an L2 reader to guess the full meaning of a word. A clear sense of a word's full meaning can only be reached via repeated encounters in different contexts. In a word, a certain amount of vocabulary capacity is an necessity in second or foreign language acquisition. Learning, memorizing and application of vocabulary runs through the whole process of language learning for students.

According to the Basic Requirements in the College English Syllabus (1999), Chinese university students should have a vocabulary of 4,200 words and be able to read ordinary English newspapers and magazines and communicate in English. While in the latest 2004 version of College English Curriculum Requirements, students are expected to acquire a total of 4,500 words and 700 phrases for College English Test Band 4 (CET-4), 6,000 words for CET-6. Generally speaking, students are required 10,000 words in TOFEL and 20,000 words in GRE. It is obvious that the vocabulary requirement is the important discrimination of test difficulty.

Most of Chinese students have been learning for at least 6 years from their junior high school, but they still not able to express themselves adequately and fluently in English or understand what people say easily. The phenomenon is called "dumb and deaf English-learning", not even to say the application of English in daily communication. The problem may lie in the traditional teaching method. For example, in a typical Chinese classroom, what students did first of all was to follow the teacher reading the new words and expressions by repeating again and again. Then the teacher explained the new words one by one, until students felt bored and exhausted. In order to expand their vocabulary, students spent much time repeating and reciting words without knowing clearly how to use them correctly in practice. Many of them could read and understand English, but found it difficult to speak and listen to it. In other words, students are learning knowledge rather than the abilities to use a language for they spend too much time in memorizing vocabulary. Ironically, Gui Shi-chun (2004) found that the first on the list of Chinese students' English mistakes was vocabulary spelling, which could account for 17.4% among all the ones. But recent years, with the development of new information technology, especially multimedia technology's application in teaching, it is possible to get rid of the negative aspects that come from social, cognitive and material conditions. At the same time, it can improve the students' vocabulary learning.

9.2 Vocabulary Learning with CALL and CALT

With the emergence and popularity of computer-assisted language learning and teaching (CALL and CALT), many English teachers have shifted their focus from teacher-centered or book-centered instruction to students-centered or classroom-based instruction. With respect to the

new information technology, language teachers may use computers and Internet in language teaching. There seems little doubt that CALL and CALT is presently the most innovative area in the practice of foreign or second language teaching and learning. From the educational point of view, it is clear that computers and Internet promote a student-centered way of learning, and in this particular sense we might say that the teacher is no longer the key factor of the learning process. Researchers agree that educational technology can help students enhance communication skills including listening, speaking, reading and writing by creating emulation learning environments. Therefore, many universities provide the non-English major college students with language labs and multimedia facilities. The use of communicative strategies seems to suggest that the way of learning vocabulary does not merely involve memorizing and monotonous practicing, but various other activities to enhance understanding and usage. Nowadays, CALL and CALT have developed from traditional ones to web-based ones.

There are several new features frequently used in CALL and CALT, including hypertext, hypermedia and multimedia. Hypertext (Christopher and David, 2005:37) refers to links among textual items, often indicated by key words set in underlined blue type. When it is highlighted by a pointer device (e.g., mouse, trackball, finger on a touch-sensitive screen) and selected or clicked, it will take the reader to the referent. The referent might be a separated screen or so-called "page", or a small box of text that appears to float above the initial page. Hypermedia (ibid, 38) refers to similar links as those used in hypertext, but instead of simply linking text to text, hypermedia involves linking various media such as sound, images, animation and/or video. Multimedia (ibid,39) refers to many of the same ideas associated with hypermedia, but hypermedia might only use of two types of media (e.g., text+sound or text+photographs). Multimedia tends to features several media types including text, images, sound, video and/or animations.

Multimedia can promote students' vocabulary acquisition for its increasing students' autonomous abilities in learning. It can also lower students' awareness of teacher-centered feelings in classroom. Hoogeveen (1995) concluded several good points by using multimedia in language learning. Firstly, learners respond to multimedia in a complex way and give the feeling of experiencing information instead of simply acquiring it. Secondly, the man-machine is more friendly interaction. Thirdly, students may feel more funny from multimedia and learning becomes a happy process.

9.3 Psychological and Multimedia Hardware and Software Foundation for Vocabulary Learning

9.3.1 Psychological Foundation

For most Chinese English learners, the frequently used way in vocabulary learning is by memorizing. However, multimedia technology in English learning and teaching can help students improve the results of memorizing words (南朝,2005).

According to Gagné's (1988) information processing model, learning is a series process of cognition, which several scales can change the outside stimuli into a new ability. Learners receive the outside stimuli from the receptors of eyes, mouth, ears, nose, and hands, and change stimuli into physical neural information, which will be in the

storage of sensory register. The information only arousing learners' special attention in the sensory register can be put into short-term memory, in which, the information after the process of semantic encoding will be moved into long-term memory. At last, learners have the responses accordingly. Gagné's model actually explains learners' responses of attention, reception, explanation, and feedback in processing of outside information. In short, Gagné's model is about the process of learners' sensation, attention and perception toward the outside environment.

Perceptual or modality strength (Keefe, 1979) refers to individual's sensory channels through which one can best absorb and retain information. Perceptual preferences influence the ways in which students learn. When teachers' teaching approaches match the learning styles of the students, the students will achieve statistically higher (Dunn, 1988). Perceptual strength has includes four categories: auditory (hearing), visual (seeing), tactile (hand-on), and kinesthetic (whole-body movement) preferences. Auditory learners can learn best when listening to verbal instruction such as a lecture, discussion, or recording. Learners whose primary strength is visual can recall what has been read and observed. When asked for information from printed matters, they often close their eyes and visually recall what they read or saw earlier. Students with tactile perceptual preferences need to underline as they read, take notes when they listen, and keep their hands busy, particularly if they have low auditory preferences. Learners with kinesthetic preferences require whole body movement and real life experiences to absorb and retain material to be learned. These people learn most easily when they are totally involved. They are good at acting and drama. In addition, the words tactile and kinesthetic are often used interchangeably, or can be summarized by one word, that is, haptic. Modality strengths involve and generally become more integrated with age (Kinsella, 2002). Children are essentially more tactual and kinesthetic in primary grades; gradually develop visual preference at approximately second grade, and finally to auditory preference at the end of elementary school. As students grow older, those with mixed perceptual strengths generally have a better chance of success in academic achievement than do those with single modality strength, because they can process information in whatever way it is presented.

As for Chinese teachers traditionally he or she may just emphasize learning through reading and tend to pour a great deal of information on the blackboard. Students on the other hand, sit in rows facing the blackboard and the teacher. Thus, students' perceptual channels are mainly visual (text and blackboard) and auditory (teachers' lectures). According to psychologists' research, 11% information we get is from auditory channel, 83% from visual channel (南朝,2005).

Because the application of multimedia technology in English teaching supplies various video, picture and literal material for students, they can use both the auditory and visual channels. It is similar to the natural ways to obtain information. Many researchers (桂诗春,2004; Ellis,1995) have proved that learning material which attracted students' longtime attention would have good effects of the memory of new words.

9.3.2 Multimedia Hardware and Software Foundation

Multimedia CALL and CALT aims to make the transition from a teacher-centered classroom one that encourage student initiative, but the realization of this purpose needs support of multimedia hardware. The hardware should at least include: (1) multimedia classroom (with

computer, epidiascope, scanner, printer, projector as necessities); (2) abundant learning and teaching material easy access from Internet or E-classroom from university.

There are also several pieces of software possibly used: (1) word processor (such as Microsoft Word, Notebook, and Tablet, etc.); (2) picture/image-edit (such as PhotoShop, CorelDraw and Freehand); (3) animation production (Flash, Maya, and 3D Max, etc.); (4) sound-edit (Cool Edit, Wave Edit, and Sound Forge, etc.); (5) video-edit (Adobe Premiere and Jinshan Hero); (6) lecture-demo (PowerPoint).

With respect to above mentioned Multimedia hardware and software, students and teachers could have a better interaction between teaching and learning.

9.4 Vocabulary Learning Strategies in Multimedia Environment with Application of Vocabulary Motivation

For word instruction in classroom, it is difficult for teachers to give explicit teaching to all vocabulary because of the complexity of vocabulary learning task. It is necessary for teachers to encourage students to develop their own vocabulary strategies and to improve and manage their learning with extensive reading and listening after class in order to gain the required exposure to vocabulary and build up word knowledge.

9.4.1 CALT for Vocabulary's Pronunciation, Morphology and Semantics

Effective language instruction should be of multisensory training in nature. That is, the lectures include students' visual, auditory and tactile activities. Hu Hai-peng (2004) found evidence that students whose sensory channels are matched with learning resources and learning environments would achieve statistically higher academically. Multimedia environment makes it possible for students to acquire vocabulary from sound, font/spelling and meaning of one particular word.

For the activities that can match students' visual preferences, traditionally language teachers may write the material on the blackboard, or use teaching aids, such as handouts, pictures, films, charts, or even real objects in class. In order to help students with auditory preferences, language teachers need to give them some oral instruction for classroom task, or tests and homework assignments. Oral explanations should be added to all charts, pictures, and handout. At the end of the lectures, language teachers may want to give the oral summaries of the main points. For students of tactile sensory preferences, language instructors might provide more opportunities to involve students' "hands-on" or physical experiences, such as role-plays and simulations.

Students will learn more when information is adopted by a variety of learning channels than when only a single channel of learning is used. Nowadays, with the help of multimedia technology, one particular word can be learned through sound, picture and even three-dimensional animation. For example, when teaching words "broccoli" and "cauliflower", it is hard to describe the difference between two vegetables because both are translated "Huacai (in Chinese)", but with their pictures in hypertext links, students can easily recognize Cauliflower in China is "Huacai" and broccoli in China is "Xi Lanhua". Another merit for multimedia technology is that the interaction between students and computer is up to students, and computer never feels tired.

9.4.2 Context

Vocabulary learning is more than the study of individual words. By learning words in context, the learner has to learn additional linguistic, semantic, syntactic, and collocational features of a word. Watching video programs or movies in English is the most common self-initiated contextualized vocabulary learning activity, while listening to audio streaming programs, reading English newspaper or books, and playing computer games in English are also the popular activities. Online-chatting in English can also increase students' awareness of the language. Aided by pictures, sound and flash animation, multimedia context offers abundant interesting learning material for learners.

9.4.3 Vocabulary Game

For most of English learners, they may feel frustrated and boring when reciting vocabulary. Interest is the best teacher. If instructor use appropriate vocabulary games to help students to learn, study may get the twice result with half the effort. Riddle, brainstorm round a word, jokes, puns, tongue twisters crosswords, and general knowledge (or something else) questionnaire.

9.5 Computational Application of Vocabulary Acquisition in Multimedia Environment

Over the last few decades, development of communication and computer technology has revolutionized the study of language and the way of language learning. The improved accessibility of computers has changed corpus study from a subject for specialists only to something that is open to all. In addition, the widespread interest in authentic materials and discovery learning promotes the wide use of electronic text resource and text-analysis tools in language teaching and learning. Currently, this is a growing trend for language teachers and learners to use corpus in classroom for a corpus makes an easy and quick analysis of great amounts of linguistic data possible. Another powerful tool often used in language classroom is concordance, which is usually used in combination with corpora. Language teachers and learners have the inclination to employ corpus and concordance in classroom. The assumption underlying corpus-based teaching and learning is that "effective language learning in itself forms of linguistic research, and that the concordance offers a unique resource for stimulation of inductive learning strategies—in particular, the strategies of perceiving similarities and differences and of hypothesis formation and testing" according to John (1991).

Chinese EFL learners misuse the words because of the insufficient input of the target language even though they encountered these words as early as in junior English. On one hand, the insufficient input of the target language has led to the fact that Chinese EFL learners do not totally grasp the rules of target language, thus cannot distinguish the meaning of synonymous words and different situations of use, such as the collocations and specific structures of expressions. On the other hand, interlingual interference turns out to be the main factor leading to misuse and overuse of the target language. What's more, some kinds of teaching methods may also strengthen the interlingual interference. For instance, the grammar-translation method, which is often used especially in middle school, greatly draws the mother tongue of Chinese EFL learners into the process of English learning.

To overcome these problems, corpus can be of great help. Using corpus in language teaching can expose the students to real life communicative situations at early stages of their language comprehension process, and can provide an empirical basis for progression in language learning and help satisfy individual students' needs.

Corpus-based exercises, the concordance lines extracted from the native speakers corpora are useful resources, providing sufficient input, for raising the Chinese EFL learners' awareness of the structural and collocational complexity of the synonymous words. For example, the students can be asked to scan the concordance lines and summarize the syntactical structures. This awareness exercise can be followed by a consolidation exercise in which learners are asked to fill in blanks in corpus excerpts from which common collocates of the node word have been removed. This kind of exercise will increases the learners' depth of processing and hence hopefully their degree of retention of collocates.

9.5.1 Concordance as the Basic Technology in Corpus Linguistics

A concordance, according to Collins Cobuild English Dictionary is "an alphabetical list of the words in a text or a corpus of texts which also says where each word can be found and often how it is used". In the modern linguistics, according to Sinclair (1999), "a concordance is a collection of the occurrences of a word-form, each in its own textual environment". Concordances can be produced in a number of formats. The most usual form is the Key Word in Contest (KWIC) Concordance. There is another kind of concordance, known as parallel concordances. Parallel concordance is often used in parallel corpus. Once a concordance is made on a word or type in one language, the translation of that word in another language within the corpus should be stored either.

MicroConcord, got published firstly in the year of 1993 and at the same time, Tim Johns released a corpus with substantial data from newspapers and manuals. KWIC concordance produced by Microconcrod facilitates a fast search and makes it possible to print a concordance line. Most European languages can be used in it.

Concordance allows a web browser to use the concordance interactively, and brings great convenience for literary studies. This concordance supports most European languages.

Simple Concordance Program as another concordance which enables the users to create a natural language list and text files and SCP is able to read texts written in many languages.

9. 5. 2 Vocabulary Acquisition with Concordance

As we all know, many English words have multi-sense. Even the most authoritative dictionaries are impossible to contain all the sense of words, let alone the textbooks which students use. Besides, some common words have numerous senses. When students first learn these words, only a sense or two are provided. According to Feng and Sun (1999), although students are provided with more senses of these words, it is still hardly enough for students to master these common but important words. So guessing the meanings of new words is important especially when it comes to reading. Schmitt (2000) put forward that "guessing an unknown word's meaning from context has been widely promoted in the last two decades", wherein context should be taken to mean more than just textural context, however, since contextual clues can come from a variety of sources.

While with all concordance lines taken from a corpus, it is quite easy and convenient to learn all the sense and parts of speech of a word.

What's more, it is cumulative thus making learners to acquire a good many of sample sentences of the word. Besides, the process is quite short and can save the students much time.

Examples:

In this part, you are given a statement and one word is underlined, there are four statements that explain the meaning of the word. You are going to choose the one that you think best explains the full statement.

Janet had been abused by her father since she was eleven.

A: say extremely rude and insulting things to someone

B: to make rude or offensive remarks to or about someone

C: to use something in a wrong way

D: to treat someone in a cruel or violent way

From the examples above in BNC (British National Corpus), students could easily observe that "Children", "students" and "old people" were abused by "father", "government" or "parents". It is not difficult for students to guess choice "D" is the right answer.

Table 9-1 "Abused by" concordance list

any offer on the basis that some of the children were	abused by	their elder siblings. That is not the case ,
not the case, but in so far as any of those children were	abused by	their father, she will accept the offer, said
as a child, Harris and his siblings were systematically	abused by	their father, Governor George Deukmejian stated his
aged between 11 and 13, some of whom had been	abused by	their parents before being taken into care. The crimes only
three groups of children: 1 Children who had been chronically	abused by	their parents. 2 Children whose parents had given
It would seem that once again nursing students are to be	abused by	this government. In April next year the council tax
example of the way in which the Europear spirit has been	abused by	this government. Unscrupulous employers have found new
quality control are not adequate. Why then are old people	abused by	those who look after them? It is highly unlikely that
a point of order ". This privilege must not be	abused by	using it for something which is not a point of order
and the law British drug laws cover many of the substances	abused by	young people. The Misuse of Drugs Act 1971 is the

9.5.3 Acquisition of the Word *hand* by Concordance

The word *hand* is an extremely frequent word in English, and one of the stronger collocations is helping hand. There are about 50 randomly selected concordance lines to illustrate the variety of ways the word is used.

When analyzing these concordance lines of helping hand we can see something of how helping hand behaves. In almost all cases (except Line 44 and Line 49), helping hand follows a determiner (a) in a group and serves as an object (both direct and indirect) of different types of verb. Semantically, these verbs can be mainly classified into two groups according to whether actively offering help or receiving it; the first group words *give/offer/lend/reach out* tend to express the attitude of willingness and eagerness to offer help; the amount of this groups words occupied nearly half of the total concordance lines, then, we say that the cluster of helping hand frequently collocate with these words; the second group words *rely on/seek/get/take/need/would like/receive* indicate the reception and requirement of assistance users want.

Furthermore, it turned out that the meaning of assistance was the most frequent one. Among these lines, majority of them are in a positive context (aspiring writers/good supporters/devotion/good corporate/encourage/potentially fruitful initiatives, etc.) Although a short concordance line is not sufficient to show the negativity and it is necessary to obtain more co-text, while a few lines tend to be negative (frustrated/hopelessly/false optimism, etc.). Two examples from the lines are:

Line 1 But they're frustrated that most of the time, they're forced to rely on a helping hand.

Line 48 ... he probably seems hopelessly in need of a helping hand.

Syntagmatically, helping hand collocates with ditransitive verb more frequently, the following patterns illustrated in a detailed way.

First, give (someone or something) a helping hand (or the passive: be given a helping hand); there are 16 lines which can (Lines 3/4/8/9/12/13/16/21/22/29/31/35/37/42) fit into this pattern and it accounts for 33% of the total lines.

Line 4 ... and give them a helping hand to put it up...

Line 7 ... people trying to give a helping hand to get the gliders out.

Line 35 ... and giving the poor old environment a helping hand?

Line 16 ... and they are given a helping hand to ensure their survival.

Second, need a helping hand (or in need of a helping hand); there are 7 lines (Line 15/20/24/25/27/30/48) belong to this group and it accounts for 14% of the total.

Line 15 ... certainly needed a helping hand.

Line 48 ... he probably seems hopelessly in need of a helping hand.

Third, offer (someone) a helping hand; there are 4 lines (Line 14/19/26/40) and it accounts approximately for 9%.

Line 19 Ideal Home is offering you a helping hand.

Line 26 The Natural Selection offers a helping hand to extend...

Fourth, lend a helping hand; there are 4 lines (Line 39/41/45/46) and it also accounts for about 9%.

Line 46 Always ready to lend a helping hand and...

There are still 17 lines in which they collocate with helping hand with various types of words or used independently; and they do not have any special collocational prosody; some examples are:

Line 1 ... they're forced to rely on a helping hand.

Line 2 ... seeking a helping hand from...

Line 32 ... that a helping hand is available if needed.

If we look at the right of the helping hand, these lines do not confirm that helping hand is frequently followed by which word because helping hand ends many lines.

Line 10 ... still give his wife a helping hand.

Line 39 ... follow them and lend a helping hand.

Line 41 ... who are more than willing to lend a helping hand.

However, there are 6 lines in which it is followed by a to-infinitive clause and it is used to indicate "the purpose after the assistance was given".

Line 3 ... was given a helping hand ... to retain his seed for ...

Line 4 ... give them a helping hand to put it up...

Line 16 ... they are given a helping hand to ensure their survival.

Line 26 ... offers a helping hand to extend the spirit of ...

Line 34 ... there would be a helping hand to pull me up.

Line 36 ... the entrepreneur has a helping hand to assist in the early states...

What's more, there are 3 lines which are followed by from to show "where the assistance was got".

Line 2 ... seeking a helping hand from North West farmers.

Line 33 ... need a helping hand from us...

Line 38 ... take a helping hand from someone as ...

In addition, *by* is followed in 2 lines because of the passive voice.

Line 8 ... was also given a helping hand by the AMP...

Line 12 ... was given a helping hand by the pig industry...

So far most of the lines have been analyzed but Line 44 and 48 are quite different from what have analyzed. Helping hand of Line 44 doesn't follow a determiner (a) as do almost other lines but *the*. The reason perhaps is that the speaker wants to highlight assistance they offer to foreign travellers. Helping hand of Line 49 is modified by a grading (a little) to stress the speaker's attitude of "without too much assistance".

Line 44 The helping hand for foreign travellers, a hallmark of Omani hospitality, proved misplace on that occasion since...

Line 49 ... but Sami's owners hope with a little helping hand it could have a much happier ending.

The information presented by the concordance lines show that the cluster of helping hand does collocate with different types of words and to some extent, expresses the different attitudes of the users while the meaning and expression are comparatively not so variable. A more significant and concrete result might be concluded with more lines.

9.5.4 Synonyms Acquisition with Concordance

Generally speaking, synonyms are one of the most difficult parts in SLA for most Chinese learners. The misunderstanding occurs if we cannot use the appropriate word when communication. But the concordance lines can offer different collocations of each of them. So distinguishing the differences and similarities becoming much easier by using concordance lines.

Examples:

The following words are synonyms. There are several uncompleted sentences, and you are going to choose the most suitable word to fill it in the blanks in its proper form.

goal aim purpose target

A: Liverpool won by three ________ to one.

B：The ______ of the festival is to increase awareness of Hindu culture and tradition.

C：The village lies beside a main road, making it an easy ______ for bandits.

D：Was it an accident or did David do it on ______?

Table 9-2 "Purpose" concordancelist

he does it on purpose. He must	do it on purpose	noone could be that thick. How
remember: At two, she doesn't	do it on purpose	She does nit understand the con
long to grow up. I think they	do it on purpose	Another extremely brave little
I said. I did n't	do it on purpose	He said: That makes it worse
No need to apologise. You did n't	do it on purpose	Then he quirked an eyebrow.
indifferent again. I don't	do it on purpose	I'm not so sure. You're alwa
the first thing you look at, you	do it on purpose	Yeah. Did erm, have you seer
in capsizing their dinghies. They	do it on purpose	it adds to the excitement, and I
Wicked. Does he, does he	do it on purpose	No, no I mean he just looks like
hurt. She went wham! Did she	do it on purpose	Something got lost and I du n no
Are you sure you did n't	do it on purpose	To prove that you had some sor
to marry him . Did he	do it on purpose	No, it was my fault , it was

The KWIC (key words in context) research in BNC (British National Corpus) makes students easily to fill the blank in last sentence with the word "purpose", which means do something deliberately or intentionally.

9.5.5 Vocabulary Collocations

Collocation allows us to think more quickly and communicate more fluently. Native speakers can only speak at the speed they do because they are calling on a vast repertoire of ready-made language, immediately available from their mental lexicons. It is the same case when they are listening. Chinese learners feeling difficult in listening or reading is that the density of unrecognized collocations rather than the density of new words. Native and non-native speakers speak differ mainly in that the former have met far more English and so can recognize and produce these "ready-made chunks", which make them possible to process and produce language at a faster speed. As Howarth (1996) suggests that "since native speakers employ a great many expressions that are to some degree internally fixed, someone learning a second language needs to have a command of those same expressions to the extent that he or she wishes to approximate to native speaker's proficiency". Consequently, collocation should play a more important role in our classroom teaching and learning.

Examples:

In this part, you are given several phrases. For each sentence, you should use one of the given phrases that best satisfies the context. Pay attention to the form of the phrase.

make up make sense make for make sure make use of make a difference

A: Doing this doesn't ________.

B: Now I can organize my own time, which will ________ to me.

C: He will ________ the time can be used, to reach his goal.

D: Before you accept this job, please read this description carefully, ________ that you are truly fit for it.

Table 9-3 "Make sure that" concordance list

With so many major projects in hand she wanted to	make sure that	everything was in a fit state. There was the rebuilding
inactivate the toxin . Food producers do their best to	make sure that	food is not contaminated with any food poisoning organisms
Book includes a wide range of materials which together	make sure that	full and effective use is made of the video. For
in order, there's no harm done. To	make sure that	he has n't just come home I telephoned twice this afternoon
what wants do what you think wants doing. And	make sure that	he isolates the plant. Ian did come in one Saturday
iron for me? she asked, determined to	make sure that	her appearance would not let Ludovico down. They went to
this aristocratic Cinderella had to pinch herself to	make sure that	her weekend was not some idle pipe-dream. For whatever th
A child's bug killed my Dad but I'll	make sure that	his special Muppet magic lives on Ivan Waterman WHEN ara
computer. Secure the drive with atleast four screws and	make sure that	if you mount it horizontally the printed circuit board is at
S STEP Design something today. Whatever your design,	make sure that	it integrates with company design and, what's more,

E: I have hurt his feelings, I have to consider carefully how to ________ the hurt.

F: Constant arguing doesn't ________ a happy marriage.

Students can easily recognize "make sure" has an intimate relationship or collocation with "that", and it is quite easy for them to find the suitable answer "make sure" in the sentence item D.

9.6 Applications and Implications for Vocabulary Acquisition and Teaching

Vocabulary learning is an important and fundamental part of language learning. But small vocabulary capacity and low competence have always puzzled Chinese college English learners through their learning process. To promote vocabulary learning involves great efforts in many aspects. Both time and techniques are needed to solve this problem. One way is that it is instructor's responsibilities to give students to learn and help them learn more effectively; another way is that students need to develop their learning skills in vocabulary and make best use of the strength they prefer when learning a new word. .

Computational application of learning will provide teachers with authentic teaching examples in classes. When teaching grammatical rules, teachers tend to invent some examples to fit the prescriptions. But the more we know about how language is actually used, the more unsatisfactory this process seems. Paradoxically, these invented examples which are thought as typical ones by language teachers, turn out to be difficult to identify, or may not even be frequently used in real communication. This is because the words and grammar interact in complex ways and what is a good example from one kind of text may not

exist in other types of texts at all. It is almost certain that if teachers invent examples consisting of a one-clause sentence they are generally very poor examples, particularly those which exemplify grammar structures. It is also very likely that for the purpose of explaining structural rules teachers choose untypical vocabulary, and for the vocabulary examples they would choose untypical grammar. It is increasingly clear that teachers need a sensitivity to examples, so they can direct learners' attention to natural, often spoken, examples which are most likely to promote acquisition.

In doing the task, many problems should be fixed up, such as where should teachers go for more real examples; what are criteria to judge whether an example is real or not, etc. With the help of a computer concordance, these problems will be solved for the reason that examples chosen from concordances are all authentic and all from natural language. And also with different concordance conditions, particular examples appropriate or various groups of learners can also be picked up. Teachers would become better at choosing appropriate examples if they pay more attention to the context which surrounds the language point they are interested. Observing real data can quickly persuade teachers to believe the danger of taking examples away from the natural contexts in which they occur and, ever more, the danger of inventing examples in the classroom.

Computational application of learning will be of great importance in assisting teachers with collocation teaching. From a classroom point of view, teachers have to remind themselves that collocations are not words which are put together, they are words which naturally occur together, when teacher "build" collocations in the language classroom the process is artificial, the reverse of how language is used in normal circumstances. This means the teacher needs to be alert to the fact that the larger the unit a teacher can identify, and which learners can be encouraged to notice and record, the more likely it is that this language will become part of the learners' intake complete with certain grammatical features, accessible for future use. If the intake is accurately noticed or stored, certain grammatical errors are likely to be eliminated, or at least their number reduced in the learners' own output. When language is used naturally, grammar and words interact in complex ways; both teachers and learners have a strong tendency to take new words out of context. But taking words out of their natural context leaves behind important information, not concerned with what the word means but with how the word used.

Computational application will bridge the gap between grammar teaching and lexis teaching. Grammar and vocabulary are not separate in the way assumed in most language teaching materials. Observations to real language data reveal that language consists of many patterns than was previously believed. Many of these depend on the genre of the text and extend over sentence boundaries—they are discourse, not sentence grammar. Sinclair (1988) points out that it was totally wrong to teach grammar pattern first and then vocabulary to fill up those patterns. Instead of separation, grammar and lexis should be merged into one lexis-grammar. So it is quite sensible that teachers teach grammar and lexis at the same time. And Wills (1996) also advocates in his lexical syllabus that in language teaching, teachers should put lexis in a certain grammatical context. Lexis should not be treated as an isolated item and the introduction of grammar is not to tell students how to arrange these items. There is a complicated relationship between lexis and grammar. Concordances make patterns of lexis well-marked and enable learners to

find out features of language which usually are easily to be neglected thus "make the invisible visible" according to Stevens (1995).

Corpus-based analyses have led to a new inductive teaching methodology, called data-driven learning (DDL), which Johns and King (1991) describe as "the use in the classroom of computer-generated concordances to get students to explore regularities of patterning in the target language, and the development of activities and exercises based on concordance output".

Johns (1991) suggests learners should be guided to discover the foreign language, much in the same way as corpus linguists discover facts of their own language that had previously gone unnoticed. This shift of emphasis from deductive to inductive leaning routines has wide-ranging effects on: first, the teacher, who becomes a coordinator of research, or facilitator; second, the learner, who learns how to learn through exercises that involve the observation and interpretation of patterns of use; third, the role of pedagogic grammars, whose level of abstraction often works against their effectiveness.

DDL supports that students act as "language detectives" according to Johns (1997), discovering facts from authentic examples about the language they are learning. DDL involves setting up situations in which students can answer questions about language itself by studying corpus data in the form of concordance lines or sentences.

More recent developments in DDL according to Berndini (2000) speaks highly of encouraging students by designing their corpus investigations so as to make the best use of the "serendipity" effect of searching a corpus if the agenda allows and a subsequent observations that students happen across can be appealing as well. Advanced learners can take advantage of it to fill gaps in their knowledge. Cobb and Horst

(2001) describe an experiment to teach large amount of vocabulary to EAP students, using concordances from a corpus of texts from the students' language course. In this very controlled environment, it is concordance rather other methods that enable students to achieve more success in learning.

It is concordance lines that make corpora such a useful tool for language learners and researchers. They can show learners the authentic usage of certain words. The authentic use is better than the sample sentences provided in common dictionaries in that they represent the real use of the words, rather than coming from dictionary compilers' imagination. In addition, concordance lines make language learning much easier and effective.

Under the implementation Corpus-based teaching approach and data-driven learning, the autonomous learning is facing a much challenging and promising future.

CALL and CALT practice make a positive aspect in students' acquisition and give them more autonomy in language learning. With the help of sound, picture and video, language learner could be stimulated by visual, auditory and hands-on interaction in vocabulary acquisition. The material could motivate learners to interact far more often than they would in traditional language classroom. The supplies of music, film and interaction with computer enable students to learn new words in natural way.

Since language is a carrier which not only carries the information of language but also carries the information of culture, it's only through the culture that full comprehension is possible. Teachers are responsible to integrate culture and vocabulary and make the course content relevant to students' current and future concerns. The English language and its

culture are both ever-changing with the changing world. This is why we emphasize the use of updated authentic learning materials, which is available on the net.

The ultimate aim of English teaching is to assist learners in their need to develop strategies of knowledge retrieval, production and dissemination. It is important to make students aware of the processes and strategies involved in vocabulary learning so that they themselves can develop those that work best for them. Such a process-oriented approach to learning will not only lead to a better understanding of vocabulary and structure and more effective acquisition of language proficiency, it will also lead to more learning competence as well as language awareness.

Chapter Ten Conclusion

In the preceding chapters, we overviewed the arguments over the relationship between arbitrariness and motivation of linguistic signs, investigated some lexical motivations. In this chapter, we will conclude with the following.

10.1 On Motivation

Theoretically speaking, the study on motivations of linguistic signs is one aspect of the study on the relationship between arbitrariness and motivation. By further examining the relationship between arbitrariness and motivation, we find that Saussure's "arbitrariness" does not necessarily mean that "one may create or change linguistic signs as he or she likes", but that linguistic signs are relatively arbitrary. This implies that linguistic signs are both arbitrary and motivated. In other words, they are motivationally arbitrary, or arbitrary on the motivated basis. They are both natures of linguistic signs.

With regard to some individual words, some words are arbitrary while others are motivated. We tend to hold that arbitrariness is relative, while motivation is absolute. By saying they are arbitary, we

mean the arbitariness happens only with in certain times. By saying they are motivated, we mean the motivations are sooner or later to be found. This is because motivations of linguistic signs largely depend on man's cognition and knowledge. In other words, when we are in the ignorance of the history of some linguistic signs (motivation), we say it is arbitrary, and that when we succeed in tracing the origin of the story regarding its invention, we say it is motivated.

Both arbitrariness and motivation can be discussed with regard to an individual sign or a group of words. They can be studied either on a layer-to-layered basis or on a multi-layered basis. Linguistically speaking, among synonymous paradigms, the superordinate of the hyponyms is the motivation of the hyponyms, which are always superordinate-orientedly arbitrary. In this sense, they are not in conflict, but in agreement with each other.

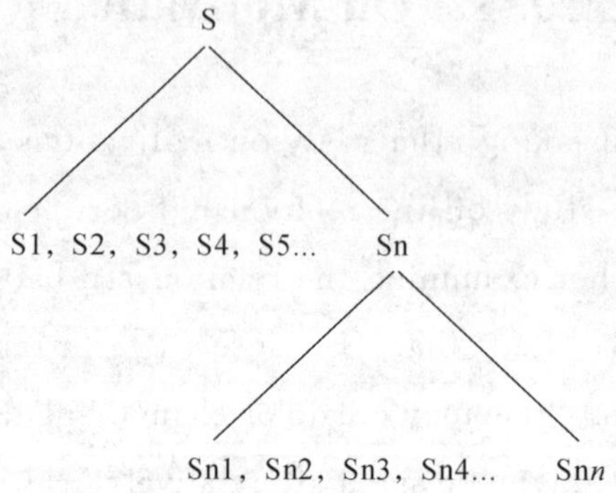

Figure 10-1 The layer-to-layer linguistic signs

In Figure 10-1, the letter S stands for linguistic signs, S serves as a superordinate of S1, S2, etc., Sn serves as a superordinate of Sn1, Sn2, etc., but as a hyponym of S.

The layer-to-layer viewpoint can be applied in the chronological axis. We say that linguistic signs are arbitrary in certain times, in certain areas, and in the mind of certain persons. However, words that could not be motivated in the past are motivated now. Hence, we say arbitrariness is relative, while motivation is absolute.

Semantically speaking, synonyms are arbitrary, but not arbitrary if their semantic connotations are taken into consideration. Let's take *public official* and *politician* for example. The former implies commendatory connotation, while the latter suggests a derogatory connotation. Synonyms are arbitrary regardless of their semantic intensity, while they would be otherwise if semantic intensity were taken into consideration (comparing *disaster* with *cataclysm*). Synonyms are generally arbitrary, but quite the opposite when semantic coverage is taken into account (comparing *boy* with *child*).

10.1.1 On Motivations of English Lexis

By investigating motivations of new English lexis, we find it is highly motivated. This is because most of them are compounds, derivates, abbreviations, loan words, or coinages. Although new English words are motivated either morphologically or semantically, they tend to be more abbreviated, more various, more influential, and more casual.

They are more abbreviated because of the more and more quickening living and working pace. People in the modern society are trying to find more efficient approaches to get more information with less effort. According to *English-Chinese IT Abbreviations Dictionary* (戚建平,邬江兴,2004), 30,000 new entries have been included, which only involve computer technology, the Internet, communications, electronic business, multi-media, micro-electronics, and military communication technology, not to mention words in other fields. Therefore, the

economical application of language is irreversible.

Words are becoming more and more casual. Although English people prefer to use Standard English, the influence by other countries, especially by people from the US, has become greater and greater. By contrast, people from the US are in favor of whatever is casual, which is surely influencial to the language.

Words are more various, because English is widely used in almost every part of the world. It is enriched by borrowing and combining with others, thereby obtaining the largest number of loans with different characteristics of different cultures.

Words are more influential, regardless of historical and political reasons, as they are from highly advanced information technologies in the US, which determines the dominant position of the language in the world. According to the *Oxford Dictionary of Computing* (2001), about 1,700 new entries are included, in addition to the 8,000 old ones. It keeps increasing, which implies the great influence of information technology on language.

Words derived from influential events in politics and society, though not in a great number in the total lexis, are more numerous than in any other language lexis. They are so influential that once words of this kind are coined, they soon spread throughout the world.

10.1.2 On Phonological Motivations of New English Lexis

Phonological motivations in new English lexis mainly contains onomatopoeia, reduplication, phonological change of shifting, and phonemes. To a narrow degree (in phonology), motivation in onomatopoeia can be highly motivated. The fact that there exists a direct relationship between the onomatopoeia and the objective world unquestionably supports the onomatopoeia motivation in words. To a broader extent (compared with morphological and semantic motivations), the phonological motivation in English words is considered very low due to the fact that written words are considered to be the major form in language recording.

Phonological motivation is generally considered as the most traditional kind of motivations. Among the four, onomatopoeia can be most highly motivated. The likely reason is because there is direct relationship between onomatopoeia and the objective world.

Many scholars believe that not all the words' meanings formed phonologically can be deduced. Yet, we tend to believe that any sound as well as any word can be both motivated and arbitrary on a layer-to-layer basis. By saying onomatopoeia can be the most highly motivated, we mean the motivation in onomatopoeia is likely to be traced upon. In other words, it is what is on the surface that looks most apparent. For example, we may find phonological motivations in the onomatopoeia *miaow*, indicating the sound of a cat can be phonologically motivated. Yet either *miaow*, *miaou*, *meow* or *mew* can be used arbitrarily to indicate the sound a cat pronounces. The motivation of the onomatopoeia of *miaow* restricts *miaow*, *miaou*, *meow* or *mew* in a relatively arbitrary scope.

10.1.3 On Morphological Motivations of New English Lexis

Morphological motivations in new English lexis involve two main categories: the pictographic motivations and word formation motivations. The former contains pictographs of some capital letters, of pictograph meanings, of initial pictographs and recessive pictographs. English, though a language containing a phonological system,

possesses, at least partly, some pictographic motivations. The reason why Chinese linguists have achieved some academic findings in the study of pictographic motivations of English lexis is that languages possess similarities, and that "our shared experience of the world is also stored in our everyday language and can thus be gleaned from the way we express our ideas" (Ungerer, 2001). The fresh viewpoint of some Chinese linguists, though controversial, is worth encouraging, for any encouragements will likely lead to more findings. The latter covers compounding, derivation, abbreviation, back-formation, borrowing, and coinage, with clipping, initials, acronyms and blending being different forms of abbreviation. The study on morphological motivations of new English lexis deals only with linguistic signs themselves, that is, the internal study of linguistic signs. It tackles the meanings or senses of words as well as the word formation.

10.1.4 On Semantic Motivations of New English Lexis

Semantic motivations in words are closely associated with history and cultures. Therefore, we say, language is the carrier of a meaning, of a culture, of a history and even of a political issue. Semantic motivations can be roughly classified into two major types: the internal (linguistic) one and the external one. Semantic motivations extend to a large variety of fields, such as politics, social events, environment, lifestyle, science and technology, information science, and psychology.

New words, related to the computer technology and the Internet, account for the largest proportion of newly coined words, most of which are in American English. This is because of the high development of information technology in the US.

In addition, when compared with other languages, the political, scientific and technological influences on language in the US are more profound than in any other countries. This is also due to the advanced science and technology, as well as the powerful influence of politics.

In conclusion, it is the advantage or superiority in science and technology that makes the nation more powerful, thus making its language more influential, regardless of its history.

10.1.5 On Psychological Motivations of English Lexis

As mentioned earlier, arbitrariness and motivation are both natures of linguistic signs. The former guarantees the creativity and productivity of new lexis, while the latter implies there are some rules for language learners to follow. The process in which English new words are invented is completed by imitating the sounds of nature, the images they represent, the characteristics of the images they represent, and the ways some words are formed. Psychologically, they are imitational and creative motivations. By investigating the psychological motivations of imitation or creation in inventing new words, we may not only reveal some rules to follow in creating words, but also help learners to enlarge their vocabulary more effectively and efficiently. In this sense, this study is of great significance to language teaching and learning.

As mentioned in Chapter Six, the way the new lexis is built not only reflects man's physical activities but also mirrors the inner world of man's mind. Therefore, language study should be closely related to man's psychological process (桂诗春, 1991). Many new English lexis stand for the concentrated form of different mental activities, as well as of many physical activities, of human beings. Man's mental activities, including thinking patterns, in turn strongly affect the invention of new lexis.

No matter which motivation it belongs to, the changes they bring forward are all a reflection on man's activities. The newly formed words, as the carrier of cultures, and the pictures of man's activities, are sure to reflect man's mind and cognition.

10.1.6 On Etymological Motivations of English Lexis

As we have known, etymology is the study of the history of words, their origins and the changes of their form and meaning over time. Very often, the history of the word can explain why a form has acquired a particular meaning. From the source of words and their meaning, we can also get their motivation. Analysis on the etymological motivation contributes to understand the source of the shared language family and its vocabulary.

Etymological motivation is one of the features of language evolution and development. To some extent, it reflects the culture and history of language. Therefore, in the language teaching, particularly in vocabulary teaching, learning etymological motivation can strengthen both the understanding of the vocabulary and the input of its related culture. On one hand, with the input of etymology of words, English learners will show more interest and efficiency in vocabulary learning; and on the other hand, learners are more confident in cultural awareness. We can draw the conclusion that etymological motivation plays a significant role in English language and culture learning.

10.1.7 On L2 Mental Lexicon and Lexis Acquisition

Knowing how words are stored and retrieved in the mental lexicon is very important in vocabulary acquisition. Researchers used various ways to study the nature of the mental lexicon and among them word association test is regarded as an effective way of studying the mental lexicon.

Word association tests have been widely applied to the L2 mental lexicon and the bilingual mental lexicon study since last few decades. Researchers study the structure of the L2 mental lexicon or the model of the storage and retrieval of lexicons in the mental lexicon or how different the organization of L2 mental lexicon is from that of L1 mental lexicon by means of word association tests. The findings show that L2 language learners have not established systematic and stable networks between words. And the semantic network in mental lexicon is underdeveloped.

The research on the nature of the L2 mental lexicon has some important implications for the L2 vocabulary acquisition. For instance, In college English teaching, teachers are supposed to organize some activities and exercises to help students construct semantic association networks.

10.1.8 On Lexical Motivations and Computer-assisted Lexis Acquisition

The application of lexical motivation with computer assisted teaching and learning will probably prove to be the most prosperous trend in the future, because it is difficult for teachers to give explicit teaching to all vocabulary because of the complexity of vocabulary learning task. It is necessary for teachers to encourage students to develop their own vocabulary strategies and to improve and manage their learning with extensive reading and listening outside the class in order to gain the required exposure to vocabulary and build up word knowledge.

With access to multichannel of information input by sound, image and video, students could have more opportunities in exposure to

simulate real life experience, which could have better effects than simple and dull spoon-feed teaching and learning methods. On one hand, the DDL (Data Driven Learning) with corpus-base can increase students' interests to detect and observe vocabulary in their own way; on the other hand, language teacher could just be a coordinator or facilitator.

Finally yet importantly, the ultimate aim of English teaching is to assist learners in their need to develop their own learning strategies. It is important to make students aware of the processes involved in vocabulary learning so that they themselves can develop those strategies that work best for them. Thus, CALL and CALT practice make a positive aspect in students' acquisition and give them more autonomy in language learning.

10.2 Limitations of the Study

In order to comprehend properly and fully the principle of arbitrariness proposed by Saussure, we read the English version of *Course in General Linguistics* by Saussure, translated by Joy Harris, and the Chinese version translated by Gao Ming-kai. Unfortunately, we did not read the original version, simply because of the obstacles of language. In this sense, an exact understanding of principle of arbitrariness becomes a bit more difficult.

The fact that there is still a debate over arbitrariness and motivation of linguistic signs makes it difficult for us to provide a very pursuing solution on the arbitrariness and motivation. Here is a mere opinion.

To be academically open and honest, we have read many publications on the issue, yet most of them are in Chinese. As a result, we are better aware of the research situation at home rather than abroad, which limits our study oneway or another.

Although this study has involved a great deal of hard work, it is far from perfection. This is because the study on motivations of linguistic signs extends to almost every academic field, involving not only cognitive linguistics, sociolinguistics, etymology, psychology, logic study, but also physics, and some other related natural sciences so that we can hardly cover all the aspects in this limited paper. The study on motivations in new English words is only one part of the issue concerning motivation. Secondly, the fact that the initial processes of quite a number of words still remain unclear to us limits this study. Whether we can achieve more on this study largely depends on man's cognition. Furthermore, the types of motivations listed in this study are by no means exhaustive. Motivations involve the internal and external motivations of linguistic signs, of linguistic forms, styles and contents, etc. Motivations extend not only to science of human but also to science of nature. It deserves a life-long exploration or even plus the work of the next generation to more fully explain or hypothesize this issue.

Meanwhile, as a full-fledged subject, it should not be confined to a certain language. Instead, it should involve at least some typical samples of several languages. However, as English teachers, we could only cover one or two aspects of new English lexis, for any attempt to investigate other related subjects involves group work and long term planning. It deserves further investigation in later study. All the problems above limit this study.

附录1:词典类文献汇编

1. 陈鑫源. 大学英语文化背景词典(*College English Dictionary of Culture Notes*).上海:上海交通大学出版社,2000.
2. 陆谷孙. 英汉大词典(*The English-Chinese Dictionary*). 上海:上海译文出版社,1993.
3. 陆国强. 新世纪英语新词语双解词典(*The New Century Dictionary of English Neologisms with Chinese Translation*). 上海:上海外语教育出版社,2000.
4. 王文昌. 英语搭配大词典(*A Dictionary of English Collocations*). 南京:江苏教育出版社,1988.
5. 在线英语词典(Online English Dictionary), http://reader. skybig. net/ english2english_dics. php?
6. Ayto, John. *Twentieth Century Words*. Beijing: Foreign Language Teaching and Research Press, 2002.
7. Dalgish, Gerard M. *Random House Webster's Dictionary of American English*. Beijing: Foreign Language Teaching and Research Press, 1997.
8. Knowles, Elizabeth & Elliott, Julia. *The Oxford Dictionary of New Words*. Oxford: Oxford University Press, 1998.
9. Mckean, E. *The Oxford Essential Dictionary of New Words*. New York: The Berkley Publishing Group, 2003.

附录2:英语词汇学类文献汇编

1. 何善芬. 英汉语言对比研究 (*Contrastive Studies of English and Chinese Languages*). 上海:上海外语教育出版社,2002.
2. 李冰梅. 英语词汇学习教程 (*A Text Book for English Vocabulary*). 北京:北京大学出版社,2005.
3. 李平武. 英语词缀与英语派生词 (*English Affixes and How to Use Them to Decipher English Derivatives*). 北京:外语教学与研究出版社,2002.
4. 林福美. 现代英语词汇学 (*Modern English Lexicology*). 合肥:安徽教育出版社,1984.
5. 陆国强. 现代英语词汇学(*Modern English Lexicology*). 上海:上海外语教育出版社,1999.
6. 马秉义. 英语词汇系统简论 (*An Introduction to the English Vocabulary System*). 北京:气象出版社,2004.
7. 戚建平,邬江兴. 英汉信息技术缩略语大词典(*English-Chinese IT Abbreviations Dictionary*). 北京:国防工业出版社,2004.
8. 汪榕培,卢晓娟. 英语词汇学教程 (*A Survey of English lexicology*). 上海:上海外语教育出版社,1997.
9. 汪榕培. 英语词汇探胜 (*Gems of English Lexicology*). 上海:上海外语教育出版社,1999.

10. 汪榕培. 英语词汇学研究 (*Studies in English Lexicology*),上海:上海外语教育出版社,2000.

11. 汪榕培."英语词汇学:历史和现状". 外语研究,2001(1).

12. 汪榕培."英语新词的认知语言学研究——漫谈英语中的'911'词汇". 华东船舶工业学院学报,2003(3).

13. 文旭."词汇空缺的发现程序和认知理据". 四川外语学院学报,2003(3).

14. 谢屏等."试析'美国人自己创造的新词'及其翻译". 上海翻译,2005(3).

15. 杨良生,秦大维. 现代英语词汇学导论. 郑州:河南人民出版社,1991.

16. 张韵斐. 现代英语词汇学概论 (*An Introduction to Modern English Lexicology*)(第二版). 北京:北京师范大学出版社,1987.

17. Bloomfield, Leonard. *Language*. London: George Allen & Unwin Ltd, 1935.

18. Coady, J. & Huckin, T. *Second Language Vocabulary Acquisition*. Shanghai: Shanghai Foreign Education Press, 2001.

19. Feng, Shi-mei. *English Lexicology*. Beijing: China Water Power Press, 2002.

20. Hatch, E & C. Brown. *Vocabulary, Semantics and Language Education*. Beijing: Foreign Language Teaching and Research Press, 2001.

21. Jackson, H. *Words, Meaning and Vocabulary: An Introduction to Modern English Lexicology*. Trowbridge: The Cromwell Press, 2000.

22. Lin, Cheng-zhang & Liu, Shi-ping. *An Introduction to English Lexicology*. Wuhan: Wuhan University Press, 2005.

23. Nattinger, J. R. & J. S. DeCarrico. *Lexical Phrases and*

Language Teaching. Shanghai: Shanghai Foreign Education Press, 2000.

24. Nation, I. S. P. *Teaching and Learning Vocabulary*. Beijing: Foreign Language Teaching and Research Press, 2004.
25. Schmitt, N. & M. McCarthy. *Vocabulary: Description, Acquisition and Pedagogy*. Shanghai: Shanghai Foreign Language Education Press, 2002.
26. Ullman S. *Semantics: An Introduction to the Science of Meaning*. Oxford: Basil Blackwell, 1962.
27. Ungerer F. & H. J. Schmid. *An Introduction to Cognitive Linguistics*. Beijing: Foreign Language Teaching and Research Press, 2001.
28. Wang, De-chun. *Studies in Lexicology*. Jinan: Shandong Education Press, 1983.
29. Yu, Jie. *English Changes in Progress*. Beijing: Foreign Language Teaching and Research Press, 2005.

附录3:语言符号任意性、理据性研究类文献汇编

1. 布达哥夫(著). 石安石(译). "符号—意义—事物(现象)". 国外语言学研究,1981(1).
2. 岑麒祥. "瑞士著名语言学家索绪尔和他的名著《普通语言学教程》". 国外语言学,1980(1).
3. 方光寿. "评索绪尔的语言和言语的区分",1959. 方光寿语言学论文集. 北京:商务印书馆,1997.
4. 方光寿. "涂尔干的社会学与索绪尔的语言理论",1959. 方光寿语言学论文集. 北京:商务印书馆,1997.
5. 方光寿. "索绪尔《一般语言学教程》选讲",1962—1963. 方光寿语言学论文集. 北京:商务印书馆,1997.
6. 费尔迪南·德·索绪尔(著). 普通语言学教程. 高名凯译. 北京:商务印书馆,1880.
7. 高名凯. "论语言和言语". 中国语文,1960(2).
8. 高名凯. 语言论. 北京:商务印书馆,1963.
9. 高名凯. "德·索绪尔和他的《普通语言学教程》". 见:语言学论丛(六). 北京:商务印书馆,1980.
10. 桂灿昆. "索绪尔的语言学理论简述". 外语教学与研究,1961(4).
11. 桂灿昆, "索绪尔思想对美国结构语言学派的影响". 中山大学学报,

1963(3).

12. 桂诗春."认知和语言". 外语教学与研究,1991(3).
13. 郭鸿."索绪尔的语言符号任意性原则是正确的". 语言文字应用,1995(2):73-76.
14. 郭鸿."索绪尔的语言符号任意性原则是否成立？——与王寅教授商榷". 外语研究,2001(1).
15. 李葆嘉."语言学大师之谜和心理索绪尔". 见:赵蓉晖. 索绪尔研究在中国. 北京:商务印书馆, 2005.
16. 刘耀武."论索绪尔的语言哲学". 外语论丛,1981(1).
17. 刘耀武."索绪尔对乔姆斯基的影响". 外语论丛,1984(1).
18. 卢丹怀."试论索绪尔对传统语法的批评". 现代外语,1983(3).
19. Tullio de Mauro, 陈振尧."索绪尔《普通语言学教程》评注". 国外语言学,1983(4).
20. 聂志平."异质中的同质区分——论索绪尔语言理论中言语、语言的区分与正确理解". 苏州大学学报,1987(4).
21. 潘庆云."索绪尔为现代语言学奠定了基础——评介《普通语言学教程》". 浙江师范学院学报,1984(1).
22. 裴文. 索绪尔:本真状态及其张力 (*Saussure: The Authentic Feature and Its Tension*). 北京:商务印书馆,2003.
23. 契柯巴瓦(苏)(著)."评索绪尔的语言学说". 白兆麟(译). 淮北煤炭师范学院学报,1983(4).
24. 钱冠连."有理据的范畴化过程——语言理论研究中的原创性". 外语与外语教学,2001(10).
25. 任小波."现代索绪尔语言学理论的重要资料——介绍索绪尔《普通语言学教程》手稿来源". 外国语言教学资料报道,1983(2).
26. 森德斯(著)."索绪尔语言学思想的形成". 潘丽珍(译). 教学研究,1984(1).
27. 申小龙.《普通语言学教程》精读——汉语言文学原典精读系列. 上

海:复旦大学出版社,2005.

28. 索振羽."德 · 索绪尔的语言价值理论". 新疆大学学报,1983(2).

29. 王艾录,司富珍(著),立方(序,2001). 语言理据研究(*A Study on Linguistic Motivations*). 北京:中国社会科学出版社,2002.

30. 王逢鑫. 英汉比较语义学(*English-Chinese Comparative Semantics*). 北京:外文出版社,2003.

31. 王寅."中西语义理论对比的再思考". 外语与外语教学,2003(5).

32. 王寅."象似性辩证说优于任意性支配说". 外语与外语教学,2003(5).

33. 王寅."象似说与任意说的哲学基础与辩证关系". 解放军外国语学院学报,2002(3).

34. 许国璋."关于索绪尔的两本书". 国外语言学,1983(1).

35. 许国璋."语言符号的任意性问题——语言哲学探索之一". 外语教学与研究,1988(3).

36. 许国璋."论索绪尔的突破精神". 见:论语言和语言学. 北京:商务印书馆,2001.

37. 徐鹏."英语变化与英美社会——现代英语变化原因刍议". 见:顾嘉祖,陆日升. 语言与文化. 上海:上海外语教育出版社,2002.

38. 徐思益."论语言的共时性和历时性". 新疆大学学报,1980(1).

39. 徐志民."索绪尔的语言理论". 复旦学报,1980(增刊).

40. 徐志民."索绪尔研究的阶段". 语言现代化,1983(2).

41. 徐志民."索绪尔语言理论在中国". 语文导报,1986(3).

42. 向明友."索绪尔语言理论的经济学背景",1980. 见:赵蓉晖.索绪尔研究在中国. 北京:商务印书馆,2005.

43. 严辰松."语言理据探究". 解放军外国语学院学报,2000(6).

44. 杨茂勋."索绪尔的共时语言理论"(上、下). 集美师专学报,1986(2—3).

45. 张克定."语言符号衍生义理据探索"(Motivations for Derived Meanings

of Linguistic Signs). 解放军外国语学院学报，2001(6).

46. 张绍杰. 语言符号任意性研究——索绪尔语言哲学思想探索. 上海：上海外语教育出版社，2004.

47. 周忆宁. "班维尼斯特对发展索绪尔的普通语言学所做的贡献". 现代外语，1985(3).

48. 朱永生. "论语言符号的任意性与象似性". 外语教学与研究，2002(1).

49. Halliday, M. A. K. *Language as Social Semiotic*. London: Edward Arnold, 1978.

50. Halliday, M. A. K. *An Introduction to Functional Grammar*. London: Edward Arnold, 1985.

51. Holdcroft. *Language and the Origin of Semiotics*. http://cogprints.org/3113/01/semiosis.htm.

52. Hu, Zhuang-lin: Linguistics. *A Course Book*. Beijing: Beijing University Press, 2001.

53. Li, Yong-zhong. *A Cognitive Approach to Metonymy in Language*. Shanghai: Donghua University Press, 2004.

54. Nöth, W. (ed.) *Handbook of Semiotics*. Bloomington/Indianapolis: Indiana University Press, 1990.

55. Peirce, C. S. Logic as semiotic: the theory of signs. In: R. E. Innis (ed.). *Semiotics*. London: Hutchinson, 1985.

56. Saussure, F. de. *Course in General Linguistics*. Edited and Translated by Roy Harris. Beijing: Foreign Language Teaching and Research Press, 2001.

57. Ullman, S. *Semantics: An Introduction to the Science of Meaning*. Oxford: Basil Blackwell, 1962.

58. Ungerer, F. & Schmid, Helmut J. *An Introduction to Cognitive Linguistics*. Beijing: Foreign Language Teaching and Research

Press, 2001.

59. Wittgenstein, L. *Philosophical Investigations*. Translated by G. E. M. Anscombe. New York: Macmillan, 1953.

60. Wright, E. L. Arbitrariness and motivation: a new theory. *Foundations of Language*, 1976(14): 505-523.

附录 4:词源学类文献汇编

1. 高克毅,高克永.最新通俗美语词典(*A New Dictionary of Idiomatic American English*).北京:北京大学出版社,2006.

2. 赫伯特·萨克利夫,哈罗德·伯曼.美国词语的掌故.北京:中国对外翻译出版公司,1983.

3. 何克勇.英语词源浅析——记忆词汇新途径.北京:清华大学出版社,2005.

4. 刘光炜.美国常用成语及短语词典.北京:商务印书馆国际有限公司,1995.

5. 陆国强.现代英语词汇学.上海:上海外语教育出版社,1983.

6. 约翰编著.当代美国短语习语词典.楚向群等编译.北京:外文出版社,2003.

7. 王启龙,邓小永.英语词汇源趣.贵阳:贵州教育出版社,1990.

8. 张志毅.词的理据.语言教学与研究,1990.

9. 庄和诚.英语词源趣谈.上海:上海外语教学与研究出版社,1998.

10. Funk, Wilfred. *Word Origins and Their Romantic Stories*. New York: Grosset & Dunlap, 1950.

11. Hendrickson, Robert. *The Facts on File Encyclopedia of Word and Phrase Origins*. New York: Happer Collins, 1992.

12. Ilson, Robert. Etymological information: can it help our students?

English Language Teaching Journal, 1983,37(1):76-82.

13. McCarthy, M. *Vocabulary*. Oxford: Oxford University Press, 1990.
14. Mencken, H. L. *The American Language*. New York: Knopf, 1962.
15. Pierson, D. Hervert. Using Etymology in the Classroom. *English Language Teaching Journal*, 1989(43):57-63.
16. Safire, William. *On language*. New York: Times Books, 1980.
17. Safire, William. *Coming to Terms*. New York: Doubleday, 1991.
18. Sara, Tulloch. *The Oxford Dictionary of New Words: A Popular Guide to Words in the News*. Oxford: Oxford University Press, 1991.
19. Stephen, Glazier. *Word Menu*. New York: Random House, 1992.
20. Vanoni, Marvin. *Great Expression: How Our Favorite Words and Phrases Have Come to Mean What They Mean*. New York: Morrow, 1989.

附录 5：二语心理词汇与词汇习得文献汇编

1. 张淑静.“从反应类型看词汇习得”. 外语教学与研究，2003(4).
2. 张淑静.“重组二语心理词汇”. 四川外语学院学报，2004(4).
3. Aitchison，J. *Words in the Mind：An Introduction to the Mental Lexicon* . Oxford：Basil Blackwell，1987.
4. Bock，K. & W. Levelt. Language production：grammatical encoding. In M. A. Gemsbacher (ed.). *Handbook of Psycholinguistics*. San Diego：Academic Press，1994：945-984.
5. Carroll，David W. *Psychology of Language*. Beijing：Foreign Language Teaching and Research Press，2000.
6. Channel，J. Psycholinguistic consideration in the study of L2 vocabulary acquisition. In：R. Carter and M. McCarthy (eds.). *Vocabulary and Language Teaching*. London：Longman，1988.
7. Collins，A. M. & E. F. Loftus. A spreading activation theory of semantic processing. *Psychological Review*，1975，82(6)：407-428.
8. Collins，A. M. & M. R. Quillian. Retrieval time from semantic memory. *Journal of Verbal Learning and Verbal Behavior*，1969 (8)：240-247.
9. De Bot，K.，T. S. Paribakht & M. B. Wesche. Toward a lexical

processing model for the study of second language vocabulary acquisition: evidence from ESL reading. *SSLA*, 1997(19):309-329.

10. Fay, D. & Cutler, A. Malapropisms and the structure of the mental lexicon. *Linguistic Inquiry*, 1977(8): 505-520.
11. Fitzpatrick, T. Habits and rabbits: word associations and the L2 lexicon. *EUROSLA Yearbook*, 2006(6):121-46.
12. Fitzpatrick, T. Word association patterns: unpacking the assumptions. *International Journal of Applied Linguistics*, 2007 (17):319-331.
13. Freedman, D. G. & E. Loftus. Retrieval of words from long-term memory. *Journal of Verbal Learning and Verbal Behavior*, 1971 (10):107-115.
14. Fromklin, V. The Non-anomalous nature of anomalous utterances. *Language*, 1971(47):27-52.
15. Garman, M. *Psycholinguistics*. Cambridge: Cambridge University Press, 1990.
16. Jiang, N. Lexical representation and development in a second language. *Applied Linguistics*, 2000.
17. Kent, G. H. & Romanoff, A. S. A study of association in insanity. *American Journal of Insanity*, 1910(67):37-96.
18. Kruse, H., Pinehurst, J. & Sherwood Smith, M. A multiple word association probe in second language acquisition research. *Studies of Second Language Acquisition*, 1987(9):141-154.
19. Lambert, Wallace. E. Developmental aspect of second language acquisition: Associational fluency, stimulus provocativeness and word order influence. *The Journal of Social Psychology*, 1956 (43):83-89.
20. Laufer, B. The development of passive and active vocabulary in a

second language: same or different. *Applied Linguistics*, 1998(19): 255-271.

21. Laufer, B. A. A factor of difficulty in vocabulary learning: deceptive transparency. In: P. Nation and R. Carter (eds.). *Vocabulary Acquisition*. Amsterdam: Free University Press, 1989.
22. Lemmon, C. R. & Gagging, J. P. The measurement of bilingualism and its relationship to cognitive ability. *Applied Psycholinguistics*, 1989(10): 133-155.
23. Levelt, W. *Speaking: From Intention to Articulation*. Cambridge, Mass: MIT Press, 1989.
24. Mara, P. Word associations in a foreign language: a report on the bareback vocabulary project. *Nottingham Linguistic Circular*, 1983 (11): 29-38.
25. Mara, P. Learners' associations in French. *Interlanguage Studies Bulletin*, 1978(3): 192-211.
26. Maréchal, C. *The Bilingual Lexicon: Study of French and English Word Association Responses of Advanced Learners of French Unpublished dissertation*. Dublin: University of Dublin, 1995.
27. McCarthy, M. *Vocabulary*. Oxford: Oxford University Press, 1990.
28. Meara, P. Network structures and vocabulary acquisition in a foreign language. In: P. Arnaud and H. Béjoint (eds.). *Vocabulary and Applied Linguistics*. London: Macmillan, 1992.
29. Namei, S. Bilingual lexical development: a persian-swedish word association study. *International Journal of Applied Linguistics*, 2004(3), 363-387.
30. Nation, I. S. P. *Learning Vocabulary in Another Language*. Cambridge: Cambridge University Press, 2001.

31. Nunan, D. *Language Teaching Methodology Hertfordshire.* Prentice Hall International, 1991.

32. O'Gorman, E. *An Investigation of the Mental Lexicon of Second Language Learners.* Teanga: The Irish Yearbook of Applied Linguistics, 1996(16): 15-31.

33. Perfetti, C. A., L. C. Bell. & S. M. Delaney. Automatic (prelexical) phonetic activation in silent word reading: evidence from backward masking. *Journal of Memory & Language*, 1988 (27): 59-70.

34. Perfetti, C. A. & Zhang, S. *Very early phonological activation in Chinese reading.* Journal of Experimental Psychology: Learning, Memory, and Cognition, 1995(21): 24-33.

35. Richards, J. C. & Schmidt, R. *Longman Dictionary of Language Teaching and Applied Linguistics (3rd ed.).* London: Longman (Pearson Education), 2002.

36. Singleton, D. *Exploring the Second Language Mental Lexicon.* Cambridge: Cambridge University, 1999.

37. Snodgrass, J. G. & Vanderwart, M. A standardized set of 260 pictures: norms for name agreement, image agreement, familiarity, and visual complexity. *Journal of Experimental Psychology: Human Learning and Memory*, 1980(6): 174-215.

38. Sommer, R. *Diagnostik der Geisteskrankheiten.* Berlin/Wien: Urban und Schwarzenberg, 1901.

39. Soudek, L. I. The mental lexicon in second language learning. Paper presented at the Thirteenth International Congress of Linguistics, Tokyo, 1982.

40. Swinney, D. Lexical access during sentence comprehension: (re) consideration of context effects. *Journal of Verbal Learning and*

Verbal Behavior, 1979(18): 645-659.

41. Treisman A. M. Contextual cues in selective listening. *Quarterly Journal of Experimental Psychology*, 1960(12): 242-248.

42. Van Orden, G. C. A rows is a rose: spelling, sound and reading. *Memory and Cognition*, 1987(15): 181-198.

43. Welsh, E. Second language lexical networks. Unpublished MA Thesis. University of London, Birkbeck College, 1988.

44. Welter, B. Comparing the L1 and L2 mental lexicon: a depth of individual word knowledge model. *Studies in Second Language Acquisition*, 2001(23): 41-69.

45. Zareva, A. Structure of the L2 mental lexicon: how does it compare to native speakers' lexical organization? *Second Language Research*, 2007(23): 123-153.

46. Zhang, S. J. *The CEL Mental Lexicon: Nature and Developmental Pattern.* Kai Feng: He Nan University Press, 2004.

附录 6:计算机辅助语言教学类参考文献汇编

1. 桂诗春.以语料库为基础的中国学习者英语失误分析的认知模型.现代外语,2004(2).
2. 南朝.多媒体技术促进大班词汇教学理据分析及应用.安徽工业大学学报(社科版),2005(4).
3. Christopher N. Candlin & David R. Hall. *Computer-assisted Language Learning*. Pearson Educational Limited,2005.
4. College English Syllabus. *The College English Syllabus*. Shanghai: Shanghai Foreign Language Education Press,1999.
5. Dunn, Rita et al. Survey of research on learning styles. *Educational Leadership*,1988(6):50-59.
6. Ellis, R. Modified oral input and the acquisition of word meaning. *Applied Linguistics*,1995,16(4):409-441.
7. Gagné, Robert M. & Driscoll, M. *Essentials of Learning for Instruction* (2nd ed.). Englewood Cliffs, NJ: Prentice Hall,1988.
8. Hoogeveen,M. Toward a new multimedia paradigm: is multimedia assisted instruction really effective? In: Proceedings of ED-MEDIA 95—World Conference on Educational Multimedia and Hypermedia. Gra2, Austria, 1995:348-353.

9. Hu Haipeng. A correlational study between Chinese college students' learning styles and their language achievement. Unpublished thesis. Zhengzhou University, 2004.

10. Keefe, James W. *Profiling and Utilizing Learning Style*. (ed.) Reston, VA: National Association of Secondary School Principals, 1979.

11. Kinsella, Kate. Understanding and empowering diverse learners in ESL classrooms. In: Reid (ed.). *Learning Style in the ESL/EFL Classroom*. Beijing: Foreign Language Teaching and Research Press, 2002.

12. Meara, P. Vocabulary acquisition: a neglected aspect of language learning. *Language Teaching and Linguistics*, 1982, 13(4): 22-46.

13. Parry, K. Too many words: learning the vocabulary of an academic subject. In: T. Huckin, M. Haynes and J. Coady (eds.). *Second Language Reading and Vocabulary Learning*. Norwood, NJ: Ablex Publishing Corporation, 1993: 109-129.

14. Wilkins, D. A. *Linguistics in Language Teaching*. London: Edward Arnold, 1972.

Acknowledgement

I wish to express my profound gratitude to the following people whose assistance made the writing of this thesis possible.

First, I would like to thank Professor Yang Liang-sheng, my warm-hearted instructor, for his careful insight and guidance, who spent much of his precious time reading and painstakingly correcting my paper many times. He, willingly and patiently, advised and instructed me in how to successfully complete difficult areas of my research. Later, when asked, he kindly mailed me his publication on modern English vocabulary, which helped me to clarify my thoughts in a thorough and logical manner.

I would like to express my warmest regards to Professor Xu You-zhi, who, after careful reading of my manuscript, gave me very helpful and extremely detailed comments, including constructive suggestions on the framework of the study. As a distinguished and most respected linguistics professor, he carefully read the corrected manuscript and time and time again took the time to call me with some valuable suggestions. His influence has made me revise my thinking on specific points, and has contributed to a greater precision and more logical arrangement of my study.

I would like to express my gratitude to Professor Zhang Ke-ding, as his courses on motivation studies for the 2002-year postgraduates and especially his thesis, entitled *Motivations for Derived Meanings of Linguistic Signs* (2001), originally aroused my interest in motivation study. Since then, I have buried myself in the study on motivations, including Saussure's linguistic philosophy, while continuing my research, revisions, and refinement of this thesis.

I must offer my deepest appreciation to Doctor Guan He-feng, vice dean of the School of Foreign Languages, Henan University, who helped me contact my instructor, Professor Yang Liang-sheng. I would like to thank Ms. Qin Feng, who informed me of the timeline, regarding printing, so that I would be able to submit my thesis to the printers before the printing deadline.

I am very grateful to Professor Wang Rong-pei, the most distinguished authority in lexicology in China, to Professor Wang Ai-lu, the most respected authority in the study of motivation, and to Professor Zhang Shao-jie, one of the most attentive and energetic scholars in Saussure's principle of arbitrariness. Their graciousness, superior intellect, and broad knowledge of linguistics have left me a deep impression and have encouraged my present and future studies in this area. Appreciation should also be delivered to those who work over the issues of lexicology, arbitrariness and motivation. Without their publications, it would have been almost impossible for me to research and complete my thesis, as all the words exemplified in my thesis come from them or from the websites they created.

I want to give my sincere thanks to Professor Xi Jian-guo, my colleague and friend, who offered me many valuable ideas and helpful advice, which proved to be extremely valuable in helping me to expound

my point of view on a much more intense academic level. I would like to thank Zhang Zhen-mei, my colleague and friend, who provided her opinions in the stylistic perspective, which proved to be very helpful in finalizing my thesis. I would like to thank Dr. Hu Jin-ju, from Shanghai International Studies University, who carefully read my paper and refuted some of my claims, which assisted me in making appropriate revisions to my research.

Professor Zhou Xing, also assisted me by contacting the librarian at Zhejiang University, who eventually agreed to let me read and borrow some reference books, which were an invaluable resource.

Thanks to Professor Pang Jixian, the dean of the Department of Foreign Languages at Zhejiang University, who keeps encouraging me both academically and spiritually, to do whatever interests me the most with respect to linguistic study.

I would like to express my special thanks and appreciation of David B. Gephart, for his advice and assistance in making grammatical and syntactical corrections to this study.

I sincerely appreciate all their help, cooperation, assistance, and understanding during this time.

Huiqin Wu

Dec. 2006